THE SELF COMPASS

CHARTING YOUR PERSONALITY IN CHRIST

Dr. Dan & Kate Montgomery

To order: www.CompassTherapy.com

Compass Therapy® and Self Compass® are registered trademarks of Dan & Kate Montgomery.
Cover Design: David Gagne. Editing: Woodeene Koenig-Bricker.

Compass Works
1482 East Valley Rd, Ste 301
Montecito, CA 93108

ISBN: 978-1-4303-2417-1
Printed in the United States of America

Unless otherwise noted, Scripture quotations are from the New Revised Standard Version of the Bible, copyright @ 1989 by the Division of Christian Education of the National Council of Churches of Christ in the USA. Used by permission.

Library of Congress Cataloguing-in-Publication Data
Montgomery, Dan & Kate.
The Self Compass: Charting Your Personality in Christ/Dan and Kate Montgomery.
p. cm.
ISBN 978-1-4303-2417-1
1. Personality—Religious aspects—Christianity. 2. Typology (Psychology). 3. Jesus Christ—Psychology. 4. Christian Discipleship.

COMMENDATIONS
THE SELF COMPASS:
CHARTING YOUR PERSONALITY IN CHRIST

GUIDEPOSTS MAGAZINE

"The Montgomery Self Compass is a very accessible tool that helps identify and label typical behavior patterns, while providing a wonderful handle on personality growth. I especially liked the segment about pattern combinations. I spotted five in myself!"
—*Elizabeth Sherrill, Roving Editor*
Author, "All the Way to Heaven"

REGENT COLLEGE

"Dr. Dan Montgomery's Christian personality theory is innovative and biblically sound."
—*Dr. Gordon Fee, Professor Emeritus of New Testament*

THOMAS AQUINAS INSTITUTE OF THEOLOGY

"Dan & Kate Montgomery's Compass Model is grounded in a wealth of resources and research. Those trained in Enneagram Typology will profit from this work."
—*Carla Mae Streeter, O.P.*

Contents

PART I:

YOUR PERSONALITY MATTERS TO CHRIST

I am the Lord your God,
who teaches you what is best for you,
who directs you in the way you should go.
—Is 48:17 NIV

1

CHRIST & YOUR PERSONALITY

Surely you desire truth in the inner parts.
—Ps 51:6 NIV

The sun has arced to its highest point in the desert sky as the wind sculpts patterns in the sand, which is all the eye can see in any direction, save for a white-robed man seated by the edge of an ancient well, and a Samaritan woman standing nearby, a water jug by her side.

She is asking questions. And giving replies.

Surface replies, that bat away insight. Openness. Transparency.

The man persists.

Still there is avoidance. Refusal to go deeper.

Again, he persists, now with home truths about this woman.

Truths that shock. Truths about her real self.

Her response?

Not defensiveness. Not resistance.

But honesty.

And surrender.

To the Son of God.

"Come," the Samaritan woman entreats the townspeople, "come, see a man who told me everything I ever did" (Jn 4:29 NIV).

Come, invites Jesus. Open yourself to me. Your interior self. Your personality and behavior. Your personhood matters to me.

Why is that, Lord? Why is my personality important?

Knowing the truth about your inner self allows you to "do what is true" Jesus says. This self-knowledge will set you free so that you can better love God and others as you love yourself (Mk 12:30-31).

As you examine and refine thoughts and actions, behavior and feelings, you develop the loving connection God desires with you. And build satisfying relationships with other people that flourish, and do no harm. For "there is nothing outside a person that by going in can defile, but the things that come out are what defile" (Mk 7:14). Only when you take action concerning the truth about your inner self can you "come to the light" (Jn 3:21).

What sort of action, Lord? How do I grow in the ability to love you and other people as I love myself?

How, indeed? How do we, as distinctly human beings, manage to develop more of our real selves in Christ while living in the twenty-first century on this planet Earth?

The first step, we suggest, is to examine Christ's own personality. What was Jesus like as a person when he lived life two thousand years ago? What do the Gospel accounts reveal about Jesus' personality that has relevance for us today?

The Gospel Truth

Scents of spice engulf the air, cumin and mint and anise merge with the dust of the narrow Jerusalem street that Jesus walks. It is the Sabbath, the day that Jesus approaches the Sheep Gate pool where invalids come to immerse themselves. A crippled man is lying on a mat near the pool.

Jesus passes by, then stops.

And heals him.

"Stand up," he says, "take your mat, and walk" (Jn 5:8).

Such an act is against the rules for appropriate Sabbath behavior. The last straw, from the Jewish leaders' perspective. From this point on they make definitive plans to kill Jesus (Jn 5).

Jesus knows that healing the crippled man on the Sabbath will result in his own death.

He acts, regardless.

With love. And assertion.

With strength. And vulnerable weakness in the knowledge of his coming crucifixion.

Love in rhythm with Assertion. Weakness in rhythm with Strength. Jesus displays these rhythms time and again in the Gospel accounts.

The Good Shepherd's Love of his sheep combined with the Lion of Judah's fierce Assertion of good over evil.

The Lamb of God's Weakness in surrendering his life for his people combined with the Prince of Peace's Strength of purpose and identity.

The LAWS of healthy personality, modeled to perfection in the Son of Man. LAWS that when taken
together form a Self Compass for every person. A Self
Compass for charting your personality growth in Christ
today.

The Self Compass

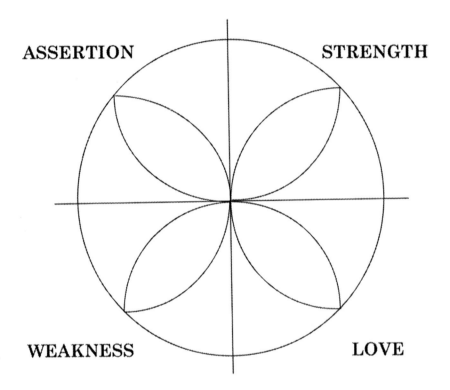

The Self Compass

The Self Compass is a growth tool for personality
and relationships validated by scientific research. The
Self Compass diagram illustrates the two polarities of
Love/Assertion and Weakness/Strength within a circle

that represents the self. The figure-eights represent the dynamic rhythm between these polarities when a person is functioning with a healthy Self Compass.

And Jesus shows us how this is done. Because Jesus' Love compass point is balanced by Assertion, he loves others, not with dependent placating, but with assertive caring. He makes close friendships with people like John and Peter, Mary Magdalene and Lazarus, but moves into Assertion as the situation requires. He rightfully reproves Peter on occasion (Mt 16:23), and sets boundaries with his family when they interrupt him as he is ministering to others (Mk 3:33-35). But Jesus is not rigidly stuck on the Assertion compass point. He moves right back into expressions of love, like inviting Peter to meet him in Galilee after the Resurrection, in spite of the fact that Peter had denied knowing him (Mk 14:72).

Similarly, Jesus shows rhythmic integration of the Weakness/Strength polarity. In the Garden of Gethsemane, Jesus expresses healthy human weakness as he anticipates the crucifixion, making this plea to his disciples: "I am deeply grieved, even to death; remain here and stay awake with me" (Mt 26:38). He continues in Weakness, praying, "My Father, if it is possible, let this cup pass from me" (Mt 26:39).

Yet with the balance generated from the Strength compass point, Jesus does not stay stuck in Weakness, immobilized by fear. He continues praying to his Father: "Yet not what I want but what you want" (Mt 26:39). Then he moves forward in Strength, meeting those who come to arrest him.

But the rhythmic swing continues. There comes a moment during the crucifixion when Jesus cries out in Weakness, "My God, my God, why have you forsaken me?" (Mt 27:46). And finally, uttered with all his

7

Strength: "Father, into your hands I commend my spirit" (Lk 23:46).

Strength, tempered by the reality of suffering. Weakness, made into Strength, by surrender. Through the humility of such surrender, the Father raises up his Son as the Prince of Peace. And King of Kings.

Christ, the God-person, is knocking at the door of your heart, inviting you to share the vibrancy of his personality wholeness, yet in your own individual way.

A Delicate Balancing Act

Utilizing the LAWS embedded in the Self Compass allows you to intuitively cooperate with Christ's transforming power in your personality.

Employing your entire Self Compass means that you express both tender care and diplomatic assertion. You are competent and strong, yet at the same time humbly aware of your weakness, maintaining free and equal access to all four compass points.

Love lets you care for yourself and the world, drawing out your potential for nurturance, compassion, and forgiveness. Love provides the bridge of intimacy that connects you to others.

But no one remains loving all the time. There are times to stand up for your self and negotiate with others for what is fair and just. Assertion allows you to do just that: express your point of view while still caring about others.

Weakness helps you accept as normal the times when you feel uncertain or anxious. When you admit these vulnerable feelings into awareness, you can freely acknowledge your clay feet and ask for help when needed.

Strength provides you with a sense of competence, confidence, and personal power. Healthy strength encourages you to achieve your best, while humbly acknowledging your weaknesses.

By synergistically integrating these LAWS of personality, and with God's guidance, you become your true self in Christ.

Hold on, you say. Don't these LAWS make everyone all too predictable, even boring? What about individuality and freedom of expression?

But as you contemplate further, you recall how, in the Gospel accounts, Jesus' behavior was anything but predictable.

You remember the wedding party at Cana and how he turned water into wine, astonishing everyone. How he broke the laws of the Sabbath for a higher good. How he always had another memorable parable to illustrate his point.

Could it be, then, you say, that the Self Compass actually offers a path toward creative self-expression?

Exactly, we say. It is precisely by enlisting these four compass points in rhythmic dialogue that you find the hidden originality of your selfhood. Jesus does not want you to become his clone. He wants you to become a full-fledged individual in him. With the compass points of Love and Assertion, Weakness and Strength up and running, the result is a dynamic, flexible personality. Jesus' behavior in the Gospels, and modern research on personality, confirms that flexibility is crucial for personality health (See *Compass Psychotheology: Where Psychology & Theology Really Meet* for more about this).

As you probably suspect, it takes effort to develop such flexibility. Because all of us, outside of Christ, function with rigid patterns of behavior that have developed over time. Every person gets stuck to some degree on one or more of these compass points, which in turn produces predictably rigid responses that we call personality patterns. And these patterns considerably restrict a person's ability to grow in Christ.

Personality patterns, you say, hesitantly. What have they got to do with me?

And, in an act of courage from your Strength compass point, you turn to the next chapter to find out.

2
PUTTING THE SKUNK ON THE TABLE

What comes out of the mouth proceeds from the heart.
—Jesus (Mt 15:18)

It is late evening in Jerusalem. Nicodemus, a Phari-
see and member of the Jewish ruling council, chooses
this time to come and question Jesus.

Jesus, as he is wont to do, declines niceties that get
nowhere and moves straight to the heart of the matter:
"You should not be surprised at my saying, 'You must be
born again'" (Jn 3:7 NIV).

If Nicodemus wants to see the Kingdom of God, Jesus says, he must surrender to the healing power of the
Holy Spirit so that he is remade entirely (Jn 3:3-8).

To come into the light of new birth, we propose, requires examining the darkness of a person's behavior
(Jn 3:20); more specifically, we suggest that it requires
examining a person's personality patterns.

And just what is a personality pattern? you ask,
willing to discover that much.

A personality pattern, we say, is a set of manipulative behaviors stemming from unconscious assumptions

11

that directly affect how you perceive, think, feel, and act.

There are primarily eight patterns that hamper personality growth, shown as they are located on the Self Compass. These descriptors are psychologically accurate, yet easy to remember. We view them as temporary descriptions of a person's behavior until that person experiences healthy growth and change.

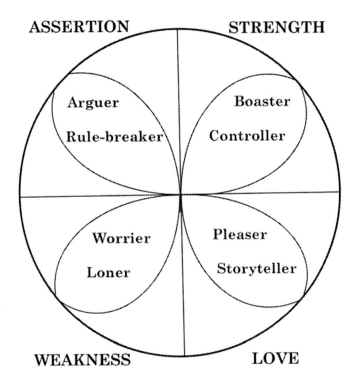

Personality Patterns Compass

✦ Those stuck in the Pleaser and Storyteller personality patterns exaggerate the Love compass point. Too much love makes them compliant or attention craving.

✦ Arguer and Rule-breaker patterned people are stuck on the Assertion compass point. Too much assertion makes them argumentative or exploitive.

✦ Worrier and Loner patterned people are stuck on the Weakness compass point. Too much weakness makes them withdrawn or detached.

✦ Boaster and Controller patterned people are stuck on the Strength compass point. Too much strength makes them arrogant or compulsive.

Most people lay claim to several of these patterns at some point in their lives. But the Self Compass both diagnoses the problem and shows you how to fix it. Whatever compass point your personality is stuck on determines your path for getting unstuck. If you are stuck in the Worrier pattern on the Weakness compass point, you take growth stretches primarily toward the opposite compass point: Strength. Over time, you move from self-defeating thoughts like "No one feels as scared as I do. I may as well give up," to "I might blow this, because I'm human. But I'm doing it anyway."

Author's Comment: Kate

I hand Dan my printed-out chapter to edit. He picks up the red pen and starts in, crossing out here, adding words there, deleting whole sentences. I bite my tongue to keep from protesting. My shoulders tighten, my jaw clenches, and I watch him like a hawk, ready to swoop down in defense of a brilliant phrase that must be kept just so.

Even though I know objectively that Dan's editing greatly improves my writing, when the Controller pattern has the upper hand, I feel driven to present him with a draft so perfect he won't need to change a thing.

Without a compass correction, this inner tension would spill over into our relationship, making it difficult for Dan to give honest feedback for fear of upsetting me. Then we'd both be held hostage to the harsh taskmaster of perfection.

Personality patterns left unchecked can undermine and even destroy relationships. They hamper your ability to love God and others as yourself, keeping you from fulfilling Christ's purpose for your personality.

How significant is the destructive power built into these manipulative patterns? In our view they constitute categories of evil. Sin, in fact.

Sin? you say, somewhat taken aback. Why?

Bear with us, we say. Then let us know what you think.

Personality Patterns as Sin

On a murky planet in a galaxy far away, Jedi Master Yoda is training Luke Skywalker to become a Jedi knight. In the Star Wars movie, *The Empire Strikes Back*, Luke is learning how to become a force for good in a world dominated by an evil emperor and his hatchet man, Darth Vader. When Luke whines and complains that the training is too hard, Yoda replies that it is Luke's impatient attitude and quickness to give up that are holding him back. Yoda tells Luke that the dark side is "easier and more seductive." The Bible confirms this truth that "the gate is wide and the road is easy that leads to destruction, and there are many who take it" (Mt 7:13).

Luke is stuck in the Worrier pattern, blaming Yoda for what he is dodging. It is his pattern of complaining and sulking that prevents him from sticking with the training. He attempts to manipulate Yoda by pouting to let himself off the hook. "It's too hard," is one of the standard ploys of someone stuck in the Worrier pattern. Luke is trying to avoid growth. He expects Yoda to reject him. Yoda confirms his expectations by getting fed up and critical of him.

Every one of us sins like this, stuck in some form of manipulative personality pattern, whether we're willing to admit it or not. The apostle John challenges every living person with the words, "If we say that we have no sin, we deceive ourselves, and the truth is not in us" (1 Jn 1:8). The sin of manipulation causes you to relate to God and others in a way that seems right to you, but backfires in the long run. Sin's effects are described in Scripture as the crooked path: "Those whose paths are crooked, and who are devious in their ways" (Pro 2:15).

Self-will, the root of sin, says, "I've always been this way and don't intend to change. I don't need forgiveness because I haven't done that much wrong. I certainly don't need a Savior to change me." There are two problems with this position: first, you are blind to your self-centeredness; second, you think God's solution for sin and evil is not necessary, because your good intentions and will power are enough.

Manipulative Strategies

Patterns	Rigidity	Pulls others to	Purpose
Pleaser	Gullible, submissive	Reassure, rescue	Get approval
Story-teller	Flighty, petulant	Dote, admire	Keep limelight
Arguer	Suspicious, contrary	Feel fear, kowtow	Intimidate
Rule-breaker	Exploitive, deceitful	Trust, rely	Lie to take in others
Worrier	Expects rejection	Feel fed up, reject	Hide from decisions
Loner	Self-sufficient, detached	Feel upset, helpless	Live in a "cave"
Boaster	Entitled, superior	Fawning, hero worship	Create awe in others
Controller	Judging, rule-bound	Feel stupid, less than	Find fault with others

The personality patterns table shows how manipulative strategies keep each personality pattern intact, unless you surrender to the path of growth offered by transforming your personality in Christ.

Redemption as the Cure for Sin

To what degree are you free to become what God intends, and to what degree are you held responsible for your attitudes and behavior? Luke Skywalker is responsible for the attitudes inherent in his Worrier pattern: passive aggressively blaming Yoda for what he is unwilling to face in himself. Were someone like Luke to acknowledge his blameshifting and ask for God's help, he could find himself on the road to more responsible behavior. While sin pervades human nature, the situation is far from hopeless, for "where sin increased, grace abounded all the more" (Rom 5:20).

In an act of infinite love, God solved the sin problem by the offering of Christ's death in the place of all people. "God proves his love for us in that while we still were sinners, Christ died for us" (Rom 5:8). Christ's atonement for sin is an objective, transcendent act of God that exists beyond the realm of human manipulation. And Christ's resurrection is God's promise made real that you are offered Christ-like wholeness when you surrender to God's sovereign power.

People can appropriate new life in Christ anytime, anywhere. "If you confess with your lips that Jesus is Lord and believe in your heart that God raised him from the dead, you will be saved" (Rom 10:9). Surrender to Christ allows you to say and mean: "I bear true guilt for wrong attitudes and behaviors—some of which I'm aware and some I'm not. I confess my need for God's forgiveness and help. I ask to receive the righteousness of Christ."

Accepting Christ into your heart does not mean you don't sin any more—rather, it means you can freely discuss your sins with God, inviting his help and wisdom for gradual growth that occurs over your lifetime. In

Studies in Doctrine, Alister McGrath points out, "Forgiveness does not necessarily mean that sin is eliminated—it means that the threat sin poses to man's relationship to God is eliminated. There is all the difference in the world between being sinless and being forgiven."

So, you say, I think I'm following you. But I'm getting the uneasy feeling that I have to do all this perfectly.

Yes, we say. Both of us have experienced that pressure as well. See if this helps.

Gradual Growth, Not Perfection

It is normal for people to think that they need to present a picture of perfection in order to gain God's approval. But human beings are "perfect" only in the sense that David, Job, and Peter were perfect. Each loved and responded to God as they knew him, yet each was seriously flawed and prone to human frailty. It was when they stood up and counted themselves as most perfect that they fell on their faces. As the proverb says, "Pride goes before destruction, and a haughty spirit before a fall" (Pro 16:18).

The perfection that God desires is an ever-humbling growth process in the direction of surrendering your personality patterns to God's healing agency. Though imperfections always remain, you are gradually transformed into your unique version of the image of Christ.

God knows the innermost workings of your personality—the motives, foibles, and desires—for "before him no creature is hidden, but all are naked and laid bare to the eyes of the one to whom we must render an account"

18

(Heb 4:13). Because Christ became sin as humanity's representative, God has patience, not condemnation, for the fear-driven personality patterns that plague people. Jesus says, "But the one who endures to the end will be saved" (Mt 24:13). Enduring means committing yourself to an open-ended process of inspired personality development over your lifetime.

We now invite you to take your first action step in surrendering your patterns to the Lord. The next chapter offers a self-administered inventory that will provide a compass reading of patterns that are interfering with your personality growth, as well as revealing dimensions of your Self Compass that are functioning with good balance and integrity.

I have the suspicion, you say, that this is what you mean by putting the skunk on the table.

Precisely, we say.

And we all turn the page to Chapter Three.

3
CHARTING YOUR SELF COMPASS

Grow in the grace and knowledge
of our Lord and Savior Jesus Christ.
—2 Pet 3:18

This is your opportunity to benefit from a hands-on assessment of your Self Compass by completing the following self-administered inventory. While this brief exercise cannot take the place of therapeutic counseling, the inventory can stimulate insight and prayer about ways you may benefit from personality growth.

The Self Compass inventory will give you a tentative reading of your rigid patterns in personal and interpersonal functioning (Pleaser, Storyteller, Arguer, Rulebreaker, Worrier, Loner, Boaster, Controller). By graphing out the results on the diagram provided, you can discover where you may be stuck on the Self Compass. Suggestions for growth stretches and descriptions of each pattern come next, in Part II. By combining the Self Compass inventory with growth stretches, you will be assured of significant progress in transforming your personality. In so doing, you will be responding to Christ's guidance for personality transformation.

Before taking the inventory, here's a prayer you might consider: "Dear God, help me see myself as clearly as you do. No matter where I'm stuck, help me find the loving assertion and humble strength that leads to wholeness. Please support me every step of the way. Thank you. Amen."

Self Compass Inventory

You may wish to Xerox a copy of this inventory and the accompanying diagram so that you can assess yourself again after six months or a year has passed. It is gratifying to see the concrete results of your progress toward personality wholeness.

Respond to each sentence with your first impression of what is true for you most of the time. Circle "T" only if True; make no mark if False.

T (P) I try my best to make people happy.
T (P) Being agreeable helps me avoid conflict.
T (P) Other people's ideas often seem better than mine.
T (P) I feel guilty when I disappoint people's expectations.
T (P) I need a lot of reassurance from others to help calm my anxieties.
T (P) I have trouble saying no to someone's request.
T (P) I should never offend another person.
T (P) When someone pays me a compliment, I quickly forget it.
T (P) I often allow others to make important decisions for me.
T (P) Authority figures should be obeyed because they know best.
T (P) I feel responsible for keeping the peace.
T (P) I believe in being kind and helpful.
T (P) I want everyone to think well of me.
T (P) People's disapproval makes me anxious.

T (P) Other people's needs must come first.

T (S) I am usually the life of the party.

T (S) I have a natural ability to make people laugh and have fun.

T (S) I feel hurt if people don't seem excited to see me.

T (S) I love talking about everything that happens to me.

T (S) When things get boring, I like to stir up some excitement.

T (S) I enjoy being the center of attention.

T (S) I feel empty when no one is around.

T (S) I'm very expressive when I talk to people.

T (S) Flirting makes life fun and interesting.

T (S) I laugh and cry easily.

T (S) At work I prefer interacting with others to taking care of details.

T (S) I have a special laugh that is attractive to others.

T (S) I am always looking to make new friends and meet new people.

T (S) I'm good at entertaining others.

T (S) I think I am a very sociable and outgoing person.

T (A) I am a tough-minded realist who knows how to take care of myself.

T (A) I feel annoyed when people don't do what I tell them.

T (A) I always get the last word in an argument.

T (A) I will intimidate others to get what I need.

T (A) Compromise is a sign of weakness.

T (A) I always look for people's hidden motives.

T (A) I have no problem confronting unfairness.

T (A) I can be pretty outspoken in my relations with my family.

T (A) I think you should be honest and direct, not
   namby-pamby.

T (A) I frequently test people to make sure they are
   loyal to me.

T (A) If someone criticizes me, I look for a way to
   pay them back.

T (A) I get mad when people don't show me respect.

T (A) If someone loves me they will do as I say.

T (A) I can hold grudges for years if need be.

T (A) I'm stubborn and proud of it.

T (R) If I don't take advantage of the situation,
   someone else will.

T (R) People only act friendly when they want something from you.

T (R) I don't mind bending the rules now and then.

T (R) I use my intelligence to get what I want.

T (R) Taking shortcuts gets you ahead.

T (R) I don't hesitate to use charm or anger if it
   gives me the advantage.

T (R) I quickly size up situations to see how I can
   benefit.

T (R) I think drugs should be legalized because they
   make you feel good without hurting anyone.

T (R) I don't mind using deception if it gets me what
   I want.

T (R) I get a thrill from breaking rules and thumbing
   my nose at authority.

T (R) A little wrongdoing never hurt anyone.

T (R) I do what I want, no matter what society says I
   should do.

T (R) I'm far more creative than the average person.

T (R) I come up with good excuses when I get into
   trouble.

T (R) Guilt is a feeling I never have.

T (W) I'd like to feel accepted, but no one under-stands a person like me.

T (W) I'm too unsure of myself to risk something new.

T (W) I fantasize a lot about what I wish would happen.

T (W) No matter how hard I try, life doesn't get any better.

T (W) If others really knew me, they wouldn't like me.

T (W) I guess I'm a fearful and inhibited person.

T (W) No one is as scared or embarrassed as I am.

T (W) I long to feel accepted, but know I'll never fit in.

T (W) I feel sad when I realize how isolated I am.

T (W) I often feel listless and depressed.

T (W) I am afraid that people will ridicule or reject me.

T (W) People think I'm boring because I don't have much to say.

T (W) I wish I could be around people without feeling so nervous.

T (W) I feel more comfortable with pets than with people.

T (W) I guard against disappointment by not taking chances.

T (L) I prefer time on my own to relating to people.

T (L) I am indifferent to people's praise or criticism.

T (L) I am most content when there is no one around to bother me.

T (L) I have little interest in making social contact.

T (L) When I attend social functions, I prefer to arrive late and leave early.

T (L) I prefer to do my own thing and let others do the same.

T (L) When life seems bland and empty, I don't make

a fuss about it.

T (L) I prefer my own company to that of others.

T (L) I like to pursue my hobbies without any inter-
ruptions.

T (L) I don't care if other people think I'm withdrawn.

T (L) I enjoy exploring the offbeat and unusual.

T (L) I find it very draining when I'm required to be
around people.

T (L) I prefer to pull back from family life and do my
own thing.

T (L) I don't care if others find me odd or eccentric.

T (L) At home, I have one favorite room where I
spend my time.

T (B) I feel astonished if someone criticizes me.

T (B) I am a natural leader whom others admire.

T (B) Superior people should be given special
recognition.

T (B) I don't mind admitting that I am an excep-
tional person.

T (B) I am blessed with many strengths and few
weaknesses.

T (B) People often comment on my good ideas
and talents.

T (B) I like to make a powerful first impression on
people.

T (B) I like to start projects, but prefer that someone else develop them.

T (B) I know that success and wealth are due me.

T (B) I like important assignments, not run-of-the-
mill tasks.

T (B) In a group setting, I like making the
influential decisions.

T (B) There's something about me that attracts
people's attention.

T (B) I tend to be cool, calm and collected.

T (B) I like to do things first class.

T (B) I know that people say positive things about me.

T (C) I like to do things myself so they are done right.

T (C) It bothers me when things get out of order.

T (C) I pride myself on self-discipline and organizational skills.

T (C) I like to do things in a logical and systematic way.

T (C) Most life situations can be turned into moral lessons.

T (C) I prefer to keep my closets and drawers well-ordered.

T (C) Seriousness and good manners make a good impression on others.

T (C) Criticizing others helps them avoid future mistakes.

T (C) Anything worth doing should be done well.

T (C) The responsible person never shrinks from duty.

T (C) I place achievement before pleasure.

T (C) Emotional displays are uncalled for.

T (C) Others should do what I think is right.

T (C) I always strive for excellence.

T (C) In hard times, I keep my chin up as an example for others.

When you have finished, add the totals for all your "T" (True) responses according to their code:

(P) Pleaser: _____
(S) Storyteller: _____
(A) Arguer: _____
(R) Rule-breaker: _____
(W) Worrier: _____
(L) Loner: _____
(B) Boaster: _____
(C) Controller: _____

How to Chart and Interpret Your Personality Patterns

Each pattern can receive a score anywhere between zero and fifteen. The *Personality Patterns Graph* shows 4 levels of response: Healthy (0-3); Mild (4-8); Moderate (9-12); Severe (13-15).

For each pattern, count out from the center of the *Personality Patterns Graph* and place its letter abbreviation at the appropriate numerical marker. The (P) Pleaser and (S) Storyteller patterns share the Love compass point; the (A) Arguer and (R) Rule-breaker patterns share the Assertion compass point. The (W) Worrier and (L) Loner patterns share the Weakness compass point; the (B) Boaster and (C) Controller patterns share the Strength compass point.

Arguer; Rule-breaker   Boaster; Controller

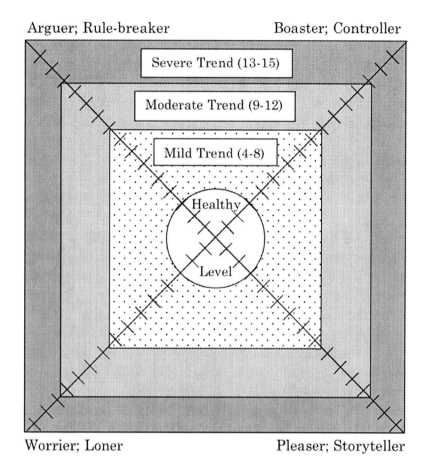

Worrier; Loner   Pleaser; Storyteller

Personality Patterns Graph

A score in the 0-3 range can indicate that this pattern is not affecting your personality. You are probably benefiting from the virtue embedded in this pattern, and functioning at the healthy level. You'll be able to

29

tell better when you read the material on each pattern in Part II.

Another form of validation is by asking for input from several friends who know you well. Do their perceptions of your behavior match your own?

A score in the 4-8 range shows the likelihood that this pattern has a mild hold on your personality ("Mild" pattern level). Through the growth suggestions offered in Part II, as well as prayer, you can develop use of the compass point opposite the one you are mildly exaggerating, bringing both compass points into rhythmic use.

A score in the 9-12 range indicates moderately rigid effects of this pattern ("Moderate" level) on your personality. This would indicate you have some personal and interpersonal difficulties that can be traced to this rigidity. We definitely encourage taking the growth stretches sprinkled throughout the upcoming chapters. So too for a score in the 13-15 range ("Severe" pattern level), where you might also consider counseling, or draw from the therapeutic principles of Compass Therapy found in our book, *Christian Counseling That Really Works*.

As you monitor your progress over several months, eventually these action steps will lead to the healthy integration of this compass point into your life and personality. You will appreciate the freedom for creative living that arises from personality wholeness.

How are you doing with all this, we ask? Any questions so far?

This is intriguing, you say. And I'm eager to find out more about the patterns. But I'm a bit concerned that I scored pretty high on a couple of the compass points.

Right. No need to feel alarmed. It's common to have a mixture of personality patterns, even ones that seem to contradict each other, like the Pleaser pattern in certain situations and the Arguer pattern in others. As you read about each pattern, you proceed by targeting the highest score for concentrated prayer and growth stretches. When you begin to make discernible progress, shift your attention to the next pattern and work on it.

Eventually, your Self Compass will break free from the patterns that imprison you. The outcome of this change, sometimes dramatic and other times subtle, is increasing serenity, improved relationships, and deepening trust in yourself and God.

PART TWO:
TRANSFORMING PERSONALITY PATTERNS

Be transformed.
—Rom 12:12 (NIV)

Now we enter the world of personality patterns, as seen through the lens of the Self Compass. Reading about them in the next eight chapters will help you uncover any conscious or unconscious factors that are inhibiting your growth.

You will also gain a kind of x-ray vision into the true motives of other people's behavior. With this comes the ability to resist manipulation that would otherwise cause you harm, for as Jesus counsels, we all need to grow "wise as serpents and innocent as doves" (Mt 10:16).

The principles you learn will enrich and heal your relationships in single or married life. If you are raising children, the Self Compass is a trustworthy guide to helping them form healthy and balanced personalities. We call this the actualizing process—the shift from living through manipulative patterns toward Christ-like personality wholeness. To "actualize" means to develop, mature, complete, encompass, and bring to final form. No human being ever arrives at total personality wholeness, yet every person can make substantial improvement in that direction. And the Self Compass offers growth tools to help you find your way.

So we'll be interested to know what makes sense for you, and what insights come about yourself and the people you know.

4

TRANSFORMING THE PLEASER PATTERN

Am I now seeking human approval or God's approval?
Or am I trying to please people?
—Gal 1:10

Eddie entered the political science seminar room and placed his books down on the large oval table. He hoped Professor Martinez would arrive before the other students showed up.

A few minutes later, the professor strode in, carrying a briefcase and a cup of coffee. "Hello, Eddie. You're here early tonight. Ready for your presentation?"

"Oh yes, ma'am. I'm ready. A bit nervous though."

"That's normal. I'm sure you'll be fine once you get started."

"The thing is..." Eddie cleared his throat. "You asked us to give our opinion about the topic we selected before we open it up to the group." He looked questioningly at her.

Professor Martinez nodded. "That's right. Your view about what you've discovered in researching the topic."

"Yes, well, that's just it, Professor Martinez. I'm not sure what I think about it. I mean, when I was reading, everyone's point of view seemed right."

Several students entered and moved to their accustomed seats, chatting amongst themselves.

Eddie glanced at them. They weren't going to like his presentation, he was sure of it. They were all so self-confident and articulate. They would just think he was wishy-washy.

Professor Martinez checked a cover sheet on top of some manila folders. "You're discussing the English versus American perspectives on the American Revolution, right?"

"Yes, that's right." Oh boy. She sounded annoyed. Right off the bat, he wasn't meeting her expectations. Eddie sank down into a nearby chair as other students approached the professor.

"Hey, Eddie." The loud voice made Eddie wince. "Whatcha doing in my chair?" Eddie looked up to see Martin standing there grinning at him.

"Oh. Sorry, Martin." Eddie got up immediately. "I didn't notice..." Eddie realized that he was sitting in the chair of the most outspoken student of all.

"No problem, guy," said Martin.

Eddie found his usual chair and sat down, cringing at his faux pas. If he couldn't even sit in the right place, how could anybody like his presentation?

The time came for Eddie to speak. With trembling hands, he gathered his materials and smiled weakly at everyone around the table. He noticed a few smiles in response. That was something, at least. Reading from his notes, Eddie presented his material. He glanced frequently at Professor Martinez, praying that it was in the ballpark of what she wanted. She seemed pretty neutral. Was she bored?

At the end of his speech, Eddie said, "I just want to say how much I've got out of everybody else's presentations. I only hope you've been able to stay awake through mine." He smiled apologetically and returned to his chair, slight chuckles circling the seminar room.

The following week, Professor Martinez smiled as she handed Eddie back his presentation paper. "Nice work, Eddie."

Eddie's eyes widened and he gulped. "Thanks, Professor." At home that night, Eddie read through her comments.

"Eddie," Professor Martinez had written, "I see here a well thought-through presentation of complex subject matter. You presented the material coherently and zeroed in on the most crucial topics, making a reasonable case for both sides of the argument. You have good ideas, Eddie. I encourage you to speak up more in class. We can all benefit from hearing your point of view."

A slow thrill of surprise and joy filled Eddie's being. He reread her remarks several times that night and in the weeks that followed. Although he never told Professor Martinez about the impact of her remarks, Eddie did begin to speak up in class occasionally, even when his ideas differed from other students. He found that people like Martin began to engage him in conversation after class. The most popular group of students even invited him out for coffee. At Bible study on Sunday mornings, he grew more candid about expressing himself. He asked God for help in becoming less caught up in other people's opinions of him.

Eddie kept that paper for years afterwards, as it proved the start of his journey from the Pleaser pattern into his unique self in Christ. With God's help, Eddie grew into a caring, but no longer fawning, human being.

Pleaser Compass Growth Stretches

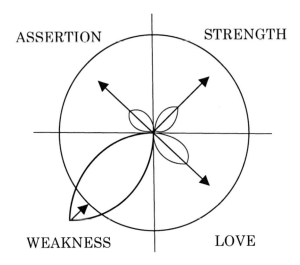

ASSERTION STRENGTH

WEAKNESS LOVE

The Pleaser and the Self Compass

When you're stuck in the Pleaser pattern, you rely excessively on the Love compass point to the exclusion of the Assertion compass point. The Pleaser pattern exaggerates the need for love and approval at the expense of self-expression. You become overly dependent on the reassurance of others. Fearful that others will get angry or have their feelings hurt, you avoid standing up for yourself. Indecisiveness makes you hitchhike through life on other people's perspectives, trusting their judgments instead of your own.

Yet by admitting your fear to Jesus, and learning how to assert yourself, you find yourself offering an opinion or stating a need with caring diplomacy. The Love and Assertion compass points are now better integrated. Growth stretches into the Strength compass point address your need for self-confidence, for differentiating yourself as separate from others, worthwhile and competent in your own right.

Origins

During infancy Pleasers usually receive consistent warm care in which they learn to expect nurturing, and form a trust bond with a parent or caregiver.

But as you begin to show a desire for independence, your parents do not permit it; instead, they continue nurturing you in babying ways. You are discouraged from exploring and overly protected. The smothering parenting style is one of pervasive control: it assumes that your only response will be to comply.

The Pleaser pattern can also develop when parents exaggerate anger to intimidate the child. You may have evolved a dependent-compliant response to avoid parental anger or displeasure. Consequently, you neglected inner interests, talents, and feelings in favor of attending to what your parents expected and demanded. You unconsciously sensed that inner-direction was selfish and inconsiderate of others. This poverty of self-determination accounts for the feelings of depression and emptiness that Pleasers experience as adults.

Thought Pattern

All personality patterns reveal themselves in automatic self-talk. Self-talk is the way the brain mulls over life assumptions—core beliefs that you hold both consciously and unconsciously. The automatic self-talk of the Pleaser pattern centers on constant worry about what other people think of you.

Pleaser self-talk sounds like this:

⊕ I am responsible for the happiness of others.
⊕ I should never offend another person.
⊕ I must keep the peace at all costs.
⊕ I should be a good listener; my opinions don't count.
⊕ It is selfish to think of my own needs.
⊕ Authority figures should be obeyed because they know best.
⊕ If I'm nice to them, others will like me.

Under the dictates of this pattern, you think you should be able to like and trust everyone and that everyone must like you in return. What makes these core beliefs irrational is that they are unconscious. You operate from one primary reality: that you need people to rescue you, bolster you up, and protect you. Unaware that you are doing so, you place this inner template indiscriminately onto everyone in your life. You assume that others, too, need frequent reassurance and rescuing. It doesn't occur to you that your submissive behavior is irritating to others, that your continual rescuing is seen as interfering, and that your smothering over-protection can be interpreted as invasive.

A Pattern Moment

Two women are having lunch.
"There," says one, putting down her fork. "I've finished my last carrot. Now may I please be excused from the table?"

From Pleaser To Healthy Self Talk

How do you become aware of self-talk? The mind has a way of emitting subliminal blips of negative self-talk.

The thoughts are so fleeting they are like the blink of an eye, virtually unnoticeable without a shift in conscious awareness. Only when you focus your attention on your eyelids can you control their movement.

Try isolating the fleeting thoughts of your Pleaser self-talk. Pause after interacting with a person, like a phone call from a family member. Catch those Pleaser thoughts like, "He'll think I'm selfish for not having offered to help," or "I wonder if I offended him. He seemed pretty low-key today."

Once aware of such thoughts, you can change them into actualizing self-talk that integrates the Assertion compass point. "I'm glad I didn't offer to help because I know I've helped plenty in the past and I'm really busy this weekend." "He seemed pretty low-key today. I wonder if he's feeling well. I can ask him the next time we talk." Instead of leaping to conclusions tainted by Pleaser thoughts, over time you slowly break free, replacing them with more serenity and self-confidence.

Emotional Life

The Pleaser's most frequent feeling is the anxiety caused by fear of disapproval, especially when you think someone is upset with you.

This free-floating anxiety pervades relationships with spouse, children, relatives, and co-workers. Underlying your friendliness to others is a sense of inadequacy that drives you to seek artificially safe relationships and situations. You quickly shove away any negative feeling like anger, and apologize profusely if you express it. This restricts your range of feelings. You please and placate rather than learning to handle the full range of emotional expression necessary to live an actualizing life.

41

After discovering her Pleaser pattern, a woman realized the shallowness of her ten-year marriage. "I've chosen safety," she commented, "not intimacy."

It's ironic that persons caught in the Pleaser pattern believe that they love others very well, thinking that one can never love too much. Compass theory suggests that too much love spoils other people and deprives the Pleaser of an authentic identity. On the other hand, actualizing love develops when love is balanced with assertion, and weakness with strength.

Those stuck in the Pleaser pattern feel lucky to find a stronger person to take care of them. The main strategy in marriage or dating is to subordinate themselves, so as never to offend the partner. Emotional closeness is established only through the need for warmth and support, that is, only on an infantile basis.

Pleasers are prone to hide behind a happy mask, repress feelings of hurt, bury anger under a facade of duty, and, if married, end up as a depressed and overworked spouse.

From Pleaser to Actualizing Feelings

A young woman we'll call Sonia is discovering her feelings:

> There's a childhood memory that seems determined to keep resurfacing the last while. I guess I'd be around seven or eight. I'm in the bathroom. I had shut the door, but it's suddenly jerked open. "Sonia," my mother's voice commands, "Keep that door open when you're in there."
>
> The shame of it. One of many such invasions of my oh-so-sensitive selfhood. And the burying

of a never expressed, but deeply felt resentment. And anger, I suppose. But that's hard to reach. Still.

I shake my head in wonder.

But with a leap to my feet, I find myself saying, actually shouting, "Mother, you had no right to treat me that way. I will close the bathroom door if I want to. I am my own person. A good and kind person who is learning to stand up for herself."

I wipe away the tears and stomp outside. Grabbing a trowel, I dig out the weeds lining the driveway and pitch them into the trash.

When you risk feeling the anger and resentment you previously denied, you are learning to be honest with yourself and others. Apply healthy self-talk to what you are feeling, and you're on your way to outgrowing the Pleaser pattern. When others show more respect for you, you know you are getting positive results from your Self Compass.

Body State

It is sad, but true, that someone with the Pleaser pattern possesses very little body awareness. You suppress physical sensation in favor of looking outward to others for how you should feel and act. Your "radar" easily picks up external signals as opposed to your own feelings or body state. It's difficult to feel like "some-body" because you don't adequately sense your own body. This leads to the dilemma of feeling like a "no-body."

Breathing shallowly from the thorax contributes to the bodily anxiety that haunts you. Sometimes you hyperventilate during times of conflict. The lack of relaxed

43

abdominal breathing deprives the brain and body from oxygenated red blood cells. Under stress, you frequently feel confused and panicky.

Pleaser persons make interpersonal contact largely through the top third of the body—the face and arms. You offer smiles and soft touches. Your eyes appeal for love and support, but typically the gaze is unsure. You don't want to give the impression that you're in any way critical or confronting, so you avoid a more confident look.

From A Lifeless to A Vital Body

Sonia continues:

I stride along the dirt path, conscious of my arms swinging back and forth. I can feel the pebbles through the soles of my running shoes, and hear them crunch as my feet make solid contact with the earth. I reach up and brush a pine branch that droops over the trail, running my fingertips over the needles, relishing its fragrance.

I'm enjoying this. Feeling aware of my body. Connecting it with God's natural world. I am here. Visible. Real. I am worth taking the time. For myself.

Perception of God

A person locked into the Pleaser pattern views God as a stern authority figure. God is all-powerful, all-knowing, and all-seeing. You obey God out of fear, so you won't be punished. But if asked, you will say that God loves all the people of the world, and that you serve

God out of love.

You are speaking the truth to this degree: your love is the conscious part of your awareness; the fear is unconscious. Regardless of how hard you try to please God, you don't have confidence that God really accepts and loves you, let alone that you are invited to a life of actualizing growth and interpersonal fulfillment.

It's very hard for even God to have a relationship with persons unwilling to discover how they really feel about themselves and God.

From A Naïve to An Accurate Perception of God

Here is Sonia exploring her deepening relationship with God as she writes in her prayer journal:

> It's still hard for me to tell God the honest truth. Often I have to write out my feelings to get past the old surfacey niceness.
>
> So here goes.
>
> Lord, I feel downhearted today. I tried so hard to make the visit with my brother go well. But he ruined it, to be honest. He just kept being remote or critical. To me and the kids, both. It hurts, Lord, that he treated us that way. I prayed for help, too. And he didn't change. So I feel like you failed me, Lord. I prayed for help and you didn't show up.
>
> Pause.
>
> I'm standing by what I said, Lord. Even though I'm feeling guilty for talking to you this way.
>
> But I'd be grateful if you could give me your take about what went on.
>
> Pause.

45

Yes. I do remember my talk with the kids after my brother left. It was a good talk. I let them know how upset I was with what happened. And didn't make excuses for my brother either. That's new. And the kids both expressed their hurt. And anger. And yes, I handled that, too.

Okay. Gotcha.

Thanks for helping me out, Jesus. I appreciate it very much. And I love you, too.

Author's Comment: Dan

I spent my early thirties as a prisoner of the Pleaser pattern. It stemmed from trying to be a good Christian. I bent over backwards rescuing everyone, being overly polite, and never showing irritation. The payoff was the accolades I received for being such a nice guy. Without knowing it, I'd become a people pleaser.

Teaching at a Christian college, I overextended myself trying to meet everyone's needs. I volunteered to teach overload courses without pay. I counseled up to 400 students a year, and I encouraged people to call me at home if they needed help. I became a servant to the endless demands of others.

After three years, a secret depression developed that I was too embarrassed to share. I resented the smiling doormat I'd become.

One Friday after work, an iron vise began squeezing my chest. The constriction grew so tight I could hardly breathe. Lethargy infused my body. A fog rolled over my mind. A friend took me to an emergency room. My fatigue was so great I couldn't lift my neck off the cot.

The doctor examined me thoroughly and announced that I was suffering from total exhaustion. He recommended an entire week in bed.

The first few days I barely had enough strength to make it to the bathroom and back to bed. By the fourth day the fog around my mind began to lift. I was only thirty-three-years-old. How could this be happening? The answer gradually came into my awareness in the form of a voice that seemed from God.

"Dan," the inner voice whispered, "you've tried too hard to please me. You've made yourself the wrong kind of servant. You let people run over you. You've loved others at the expense of yourself. I want you to love yourself as well as you love others."

During that week, the Lord helped me understand that I needed to start saying no to people's undue expectations and demands, that I needed a stronger sense of self-preservation. With those insights, I began moving out of the Pleaser pattern.

Reader Moment

I have a question for Dan, you say. How did you know what to say no to?

I didn't always know for sure, replies Dan. I probably erred on the side of too many no's at first. But my main task was to say no without feeling guilty. Once I'd gotten the hang of this, I felt more comfortable saying yes when I really meant it and no when I needed to preserve my energies.

Growth Stretches

The Pleaser pattern melts away as you practice regular growth stretches into the Assertion and Strength points of your Self Compass.

1. Practice these affirmations by saying them out loud in front of a mirror:

⊕ Today I am standing on my own two feet.
⊕ I define myself as a worthwhile person; therefore, from now on I am a worthwhile person.
⊕ I am not in the world to live up to everyone's expectations.
⊕ I have the right to take my own risks and learn from the consequences.
⊕ I can learn to handle conflict and confusion as well as anyone.
⊕ I no longer need my parents' approval.
⊕ I have normal strengths and weaknesses, and can both care for people and confront them when necessary.

2. Diplomatic assertion is an essential trait of an actualizing person. It requires honest expression and the power to choose your own way. Practice expressing your feelings with tact.

This week make an independent decision and follow through on it no matter what. Sign up for a community college class, buy something nice for yourself, or resign from a committee. Resist the temptation to ask people's opinions about your decision. The point is to take responsibility for your life and make choices that are right to you. You are taking active steps in loving yourself.

3. Ponder the following Scriptures and ask God to reveal their unique meaning in your life. Write about your personality growth in a journal.

⊕ Don't copy the behavior and customs of this

world, but be a new and different person with a fresh newness in all you do and think (Rom 12:2 TLB).

✢ Be wise as serpents and innocent as doves (Mt 10:16).

✢ Do not give what is holy to dogs; and do not throw your pearls before swine, or they will trample them under foot and turn and maul you (Mt 7:6).

✢ We must no longer be children, tossed to and fro and blown about by every wind of doctrine, by people's trickery, by their craftiness in deceitful scheming. But speaking the truth in love, we must grow up in every way into him who is the head, into Christ (Eph 4: 14-15).

✢ I am leaving you with a gift—peace of mind and heart! And the peace I give isn't fragile like the peace the world gives. So don't be troubled or afraid (Jn 14:27 NLT).

By taking these growth stretches, you begin thinking as Jesus did: "Approval or disapproval means nothing to me" (Jn 5:41 TLB).

The Pleaser Pattern: Sonia Transformed

I did it. I confronted my brother. I made my point and stuck to it. I phoned and told him, "You're my brother and I love you, Angelo, but I'm not going to let you be mean to my kids. If you think they get out of line, you tell me and I'll handle it."

Afterward I wanted to phone back and apologize for being rude. But I didn't. I held the tension. And the next time Angelo came round, he didn't snap at the kids. He snapped at me, but not the kids.

I'll deal with that next.

But right now, I feel powerful. And right.

5
TRANSFORMING THE STORYTELLER PATTERN

*Let us follow the Holy Spirit's leading in every
part of our lives. Let us not become conceited,
or irritate one another, or be jealous of one another.*
—Gal 5:25-26 NLT

Daryl is treating the gang from work to lunch at his favorite bar and grill. All eyes are on him. Expectant. Waiting. He feels aglow with excitement, not at all nervous—like being plugged into an electrical outlet. He's never happier than in the spotlight.

"Now picture this," Daryl says, his body pulsing, anticipating their response. "I walk in from the kitchen balancing this huge tray loaded with hors d'oeuvres. You know, a good fifty of Daryl's seafood specials I'd made for the party. And I'm strutting like a headwaiter when our terrier, Romeo, does an end run between my legs. I dodge him like a quarterback dropping back to pass, and Bam! The tray shoots into the air. Crab and mushrooms rain down on everybody within ten feet."

"Oh no!" Erin howls and clasps her cheeks.

"What'd the boss do?" says Hal, chortling, eyes wide.

"I'd just asked him for a raise that week, and he's the

guy I'm trying to impress with this big shebang." Daryl gyrates his arms in a Latin rhythm. "So I do a quick tango around Romeo—and then I get down on all fours to pick up the food bits before the Persian carpet gets stained. Lee Ann and Jody are helping me. And I crawl right into a pair of brown wingtip loafers."

"The boss's trademark," says Hal.

Daryl notices with consternation that Bernardo is standing up. "Hey, guy, what's up? Just getting to the best part."

"Nature calls. And you told me about it last week, remember?"

Daryl shrugs and lowers his voice. His half-dozen colleagues lean forward as one. "So other people are helping me out, right, but not our dear Mr. Hopkins. He remains seated, like my black leather chair is his throne. And when my eyes follow his pant leg up to his face I meet this scowl that would sour milk."

"I can just see him," squeals Megan.

Heads turn in their section of the restaurant.

"Hey, we'd better hold it down a bit," says Hal.

"Wait a sec, I'm almost finished," says Daryl, waving off Hal's request. "You won't believe what happens next."

Daryl's eyes twinkle and after a dramatic pause, he says, "When our Mr. Hopkins, staid fellow that he is, stands up, mushrooms drop to the floor every step he takes."

The group roars. After a good minute of twitters, Daryl waves his arms to calm them down. "So that's why you should always keep your dog on a leash when you throw a party for the boss."

Daryl sits back, feeling his body buzz with elation. Gradually, the hilarity subsides, and people find their way into side conversations.

Daryl's satisfaction peaks. The glow fades. The tingly sensation of triumph ebbs. He observes his colleagues engaging each other. One conversation turns to kids and another to earthquakes. If he were psychologically aware, he'd ask himself why his foot is tapping, his fingers are fidgeting, and his chest feels tight.

Where Is the Storyteller Stuck on the Self Compass?

Daryl hasn't yet learned about his Self Compass, so his behavior is still in the grip of the Storyteller Pattern. He is stuck on the Love compass point with an urgent need to garner people's approval in order to shore up his self-esteem.

The Storyteller pattern holds in common with the Pleaser pattern the need for continuous affirmation from outside the self. Both patterns are stuck on the Love compass point, but how do they differ?

The Pleaser conceals feelings to avoid making waves, whereas the Storyteller exudes feelings to become super visible. Flamboyant. Hammy. Sometimes petulant; occasionally glum. Like riding an emotional rollercoaster. The technical term is histrionic, or overly theatrical in character and style.

While the Pleaser is relatively timid about self-expression, the Storyteller offers melodramatic behavior precisely to attract attention.

Growth stretches into humility (the Weakness compass point) lessen the self-centeredness inherent in this pattern.

Instead of manipulating other's reactions for maximum response, you develop empathy for their feelings; their right to self-expression.

Storyteller Compass Growth Stretches

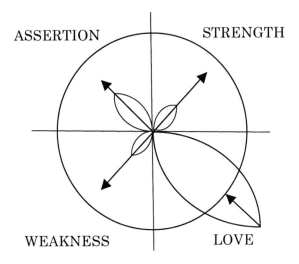

Lacking the authentic self-confidence generated from the Strength compass point, your Storyteller center of gravity lies in other people rather than within yourself. Although you desire a love relationship above all else, without a solid sense of self-identity, you lack the personality balance to create anything but a fleeting sense of intimacy.

By balancing the Self Compass with moves into Strength and Weakness, the power of the pattern recedes. When outer directedness is balanced with inner directedness, your self-identity is strengthened, resulting in more satisfying relationships. By the same token, the Assertion compass point is utilized in less self-serving ways, becoming more available to serve others when integrated with the Love compass point.

Origins

Like other Storytellers, Daryl probably developed these unconscious attitudes as a child. Perhaps Daryl's family rewarded his attention-getting behavior instead of helping him develop a rhythm between discipline and spontaneity. Lavished with praise for being funny or cute, he learned how to take center stage in order to maintain an illusory sense of self-worth. His self-discipline never fully developed, since it was based on manipulating other's reactions, rather than mastering developmental tasks.

The result? An unconscious conviction that his self-worth was dependent upon other's applause, and an underlying anxiety relieved only by people's full attention.

Emotional Life: Taking Things Personally

Not seeing any way to regain the group's attention, Daryl turns to Megan.

"Did I ever tell you how I came to join up with this company?"

Megan nods. "Yes."

"Oh, well, the thing is I didn't even know they needed a person in my department until I heard ole Hopkins mention it to someone in an elevator. Can you believe that? I'm standing right next to one of the biggest CEO's in town, and I don't even know who he is, so I say—"

"Excuse me, Daryl," says Megan. "Thanks for lunch, but I've got to get back to the office." She slips on her jacket and says goodbye to the group.

Daryl turns to Hal and elbows him. "Hey, what's with Megan today? She's cold as ice."

What's happening here is called personalization, a universal phenomenon among Storytellers. You take everything to heart, as though it's only about you. You are emotionally vulnerable to other people's gestures, side comments, or actions, because you place great importance on how you think people see you. The mere hint of criticism or inattention is devastating.

Though you generally display high spirits and buoyant optimism, you can secretly feel depressed and hollow. We recently had dinner with a psychologist acquaintance who had a remarkable moment of self-honesty. He eagerly told us three long stories, then his eyes went blank. "I can't think of anything else to say." His eyes grew large with panic. "I'm afraid you'll see what an empty person I am."

A Pattern Moment

Two best female friends are jogging down a trail.

One says to the other, "We tried marriage counseling and he still doesn't get that talking all day is part of my charm."

Modulating Your Feelings

Daryl storms in the front door of his home after work and finds his wife Emily sitting in the family room watching TV.

"I can't believe it!" he exclaims. "I've lost my glasses again. I could hardly see all day long. And on top of that, the subway got stuck in a tunnel. You know how that bothers me. I get SO claustrophobic. And Mr. Hopkins made me balance out the budget for the last quarter. It took me ages. Still don't have it right. Doesn't he know I'm much better at sales?"

At this point Emily raises the volume on the TV, ignoring him. Daryl stamps out and goes upstairs to the bedroom, his eyes tearing with frustration. Rummaging around in his suit pocket for the cell phone, he's determined to get hold of Marty and tell him all.

For the Storyteller, life is an endless saga of emotional ups and downs. Feelings govern you. Everything is either absolutely marvelous or entirely catastrophic. Whatever you feel at the moment is how you behave. It's like the base thumping from a car radio at full volume. It reverberates in everyone's ears within hearing distance.

How do you learn to modulate your emotions? How do you adjust the volume so you can hear yourself think? So your friends and family will unplug their ears and open their hearts?

It's easier than you think. And the secret is exactly that. You think...about what you're feeling. Be reassured. With a balanced Self Compass, you still feel life fully. But modulating your feelings with thoughtful reflection helps you put them in perspective. Objectivity allows you to decide what you're feeling and how, or if, it needs expressing. With God's guidance, you develop discernment about emotions instead of just blurting them out.

Think: what is this feeling I'm having? Is it frustration? Annoyance? Attraction? Guilt? Caring?

Think: what is the appropriate level of intensity for this feeling, given the situation?

Try a prayer: Jesus, please help me modulate this feeling. Give me perspective on it. What's your take?

Then: do I need to express this feeling to someone? If so, who? If I choose to share it, what is my purpose in doing so? Do I want to get it off my chest, benefit from their insight, or just do my melodramatic thing?

Take a look in the Gospels at how Jesus developed a rhythm between expressing his feelings and holding them back; between times of fellowship and times of solitude. Jesus was clearly emotionally expressive. He enjoyed a good party, liked interacting with his friends. Yet he valued his own company and spent time communing alone with the Father. Invite Christ to show you the way to balanced self-expression.

Thought Pattern

The Storyteller pattern brings unconscious, yet predictable thoughts to your daily interactions. Your self-talk sounds like this:

⊕ I am only important if other people are showing interest in me.
⊕ I only have worth to the degree that I emotionally impact others.
⊕ I am significant in proportion to how many people know and like me.

This mindset creates a compelling urge to capture and keep people's attention, even if this requires shocking remarks, reciting one's latest woes, walking off in a huff, or sharing a juicy morsel of gossip.

And when you're not in the spotlight, as a defense against feeling insignificant, you scan conversations at a superficial level until it triggers something related to you. Then bingo. You dive right in. This is called selective listening. You don't take in what people are sharing about themselves or their interests. You might say that people are needed accessories for your agenda of self-promotion.

Toward Balanced Self-talk

How do you challenge this world-revolves-around-me mindset? By catching such self-talk as it occurs in your mind. Develop more actualizing thoughts like these:

⊕ I am a worthwhile person with strengths and weaknesses, and I choose to accept myself.
⊕ I can express myself to others, but I will take the time and exercise the skill to really hear what they are saying to me.
⊕ I can communicate better without exaggeration and emotional displays than with them.

Practice this new self-talk, and the suggestions that follow, and you are well on your way to outgrowing the Storyteller pattern.

Ditch Pressured Communication

A frequent, yet unconscious assumption among Storytellers is that you don't exist without an appreciative audience. That's a strange thing to say, isn't it? Of course you exist. You breathe, eat, and walk around. Yet there is a nagging sense that you are invisible without someone emotionally reacting to you.

Shelley is a mother of two teenagers and one grade-schooler. The teenagers complain that she walks into their rooms without knocking, talks up a storm when they are concentrating on other things, and tries to push them into too many social activities.

Shelley pooh-poohs their gripes and persists in her behavior because she's determined to exert a significant influence in their lives. Now, a certain amount of parental involvement is commendable. But the problem for

Shelley's family is that she doesn't know where her personality ends and her children's personalities begin. This is known as confluence, or lack of interpersonal boundaries. Without personality growth she will keep encroaching upon her children until they build thick emotional walls to shut out her overwhelming presence.

Perhaps Shelley's husband has already learned to do this, since he reads books and watches television while she talks non-stop about this and that.

It seems that Shelley is the only person who really listens when she talks. Paradoxically, an unchecked Storyteller pattern destines you to become your sole audience. A depressing thought. But not inevitable, if you are willing to call on Christ for help, and mobilize your Self Compass.

From Monologue to Dialogue

Advancing beyond the broken record stage of Storytelling requires the willingness to move into the Weakness compass point. Not easy, to admit the need for less self-absorption, more sensitivity to other's feelings. Yet if you pray for God to grant you more humility, he will. "Humble yourselves therefore under the mighty hand of God, so that he may exalt you in due time" (1 Pet 6:5).

Jesus will keep you company as you get vulnerable with your family. Ask them to gently prompt you if you are repeating yourself, perhaps by signaling you with a raised hand. Agree to stop when your spouse or child reminds you that you've already told a particular story. Ask them something about their day and listen thoughtfully to their response. This will no doubt be awkward at first, for them and for you. But you can persevere, with your newfound reliance on God.

Concentrate on listening to the feeling tone of a family member's communication. Resist your impulse to jump in with a story to liven things up. Instead, try reflecting the feelings you hear. "Seems like you've had a tough day." Then stop. Wait. Breathe. Even though your mind races with things to say, zip shut your lips. Allow the person the dignity of having time enough to respond. Once they feel understood in their own right, you'll see a glimmer of emotional connection in their eyes.

By actively listening with humble caring, you'll begin to experience quiet satisfaction from your family and friends' authentic responses of appreciation for you. Don't worry. They'll still think you're bright and colorful.

Cut to the Chase

Another way that people will appreciate your growth is when you learn to edit your own communication, leaving out non-essentials. This growth step revolves around the truth that effective communication, like good writing, gets to the point. You don't need embellishments, emotional hype, or sidetrack stories. In fact, they detract from the very thing you want the most: close friendship.

You might approach each conversation this week with these two questions foremost in your mind. What do I want to say? What is the simplest way to say it? When you do speak, resist the urge for add-ons. Trust the power of a straightforward communication. Others will easily follow your train of thought and remember what you've said. They'll appreciate it when you offer shorter sound bites, so they can respond to each one.

Forgetful No More

Too cluttered a mind causes forgetfulness. Since both your unconscious and conscious mind are churning to provide material for emotionally compelling stories with melodramatic impact, there is no room left for monitoring life's many details. Where you parked your car. Where you left your glasses. Who you promised to meet at noon on Tuesday. When your library book is due.

This scattered way of functioning not only trips you up; it bugs the people who rely on you. They learn that you forget appointments, are usually late, and that whenever you arrive on the scene, a certain degree of chaos ensues.

So break down and buy a Day Planner, or carry an appointment calendar in your purse or jacket. Don't let the excitement of the moment keep you from writing down what needs doing and when. Learn to make mental notes about where you've left the keys, checkbook, and glasses. Withstand the urge to hurry. Instead, double-check where you place these things. At home, always put them in the same spot, as soon as you come in. When you're out, cultivate a visual impression of where you put your credit card or park the car. It is this unconscious imprint that you retrieve from memory when you need it. If you park in an unusual place, find a landmark to note the car's location.

What about making duplicates of car and house keys for those unfortunate occasions of real loss? A backup plan spares you rushing about in a panic.

Unchallenged, the Storyteller pattern blocks these memory skills. But by taking these growth stretches into the Strength compass point, organization and recall slowly become second nature. You are establishing a solid platform of competence and self-confidence.

Daryl finishes grocery shopping. On the way back to the car, he pats his jacket pocket and feels its emptiness. Suddenly recalling that he's left his checkbook at the checkout counter, he returns and claims it.

Upon arrival at home, he greets his wife in the kitchen, where he puts down two sacks of groceries. "Hi honey," he says. "I got that Poupon mustard you wanted and picked up the dry cleaning. Even got the ick medicine for the angel fish."

"I'm impressed," says Ellen with a smile.

"It's the list thing. It works." Daryl hugs her with exuberance. "I'm getting my act together, aren't I?"

From A Superficial to Deeper Relationship with God

In the New Testament the apostle Peter initially displayed the Storyteller pattern in his relationship with Jesus. Peter often acted impetuously. He jumped into the Sea of Galilee to walk on water. He talked so much at Jesus' transfiguration, it was hard for the Father to get a word in edgewise (Mt 17:5). He cut off the ear of the high priest's servant when Jesus was arrested.

But in the wake of his baptism in the Holy Spirit, Peter acquired a more balanced use of his Love, Weakness, and Strength compass points. Eventually, Peter became the rock of assertive caring and humble strength, actualizing his true personality as Christ had foretold.

How do you deepen your relationship with the Lord? It helps to remember that God longs for a dialogue with you, up close and personal. The more you allow the Holy Spirit to strip away the Storyteller pattern, the more tangible his presence becomes in your daily life. The more strongly connected you feel to the Lord, the more you find your real self. But as with any relationship, it needs consistent attention for it to blossom.

Find time each day, then, for a quiet period of reflection. Buy a prayer journal that appeals to you. Talk to God on paper about your thoughts and feelings, the way you would to your best friend—because he is. Writing often reveals insights and allows pauses that speaking out loud does not. Remember to stop and listen for the still small voice of the Lord. Invite Jesus to clearly show you how he is working in your life.

You might try a prayer like this from your Weakness compass point: "Dear Lord, I know I take things too personally and that I talk too much. Forgive me for stealing the glory that belongs to you. I humbly ask you to help me outgrow my Storyteller ways. Calm my inner anxieties and give me a sound mind. Help me to relax and become more sensitive to you and others. Thank you. Amen."

Practical Growth Stretches

1. Decide on an individual pursuit that interests you and then stick to it: a course in finances or art; reading or walking time. The apostle Paul comments: "Discipline always seems painful rather than pleasant at the time, but later it yields the peaceful fruit of righteousness to those who have been trained by it" (Heb 12:11).

2. How might these Scriptures relate to you? Invite God to help you develop emotional stability, objective thinking, stick-to-itiveness, and serenity.

⊕ Do not judge by appearances, but judge with right judgment (Jn 7:24).
⊕ Learn to be wise and develop good judgment and common sense! I cannot overemphasize this

64

point. Cling to wisdom—she will protect you. Love her—she will guard you (Prov 4:5–6 TLB).

✛ Avoid profane chatter, for it will lead people into more and more impiety, and their talk will spread like gangrene (2 Tim 2:16-17).

✛ Love is patient; love is kind; love is not envious or boastful or arrogant or rude. It does not insist on its own way; it is not irritable or resentful (1 Cor 13:4-5).

3. Do three things by yourself this week. Your capacity for healthy solitude and quiet communion with the Lord allows you to enjoy your own company. Eat at a new cafe, take a little road trip, enjoy a sunset, or write in your journal—and keep it to yourself! Are you feeling less of that hollow emptiness? More of an inner satisfaction? Enjoy operating with a balanced Self Compass.

Transforming the Storyteller Pattern

Daryl has been using the Self Compass growth tool for several months. He arrives at the entrance to the hotel ballroom where his office Christmas party is in full swing. Let's enter his mind and hear his train of thought:

Scanning the crowd, I adjust the knot in my red Rudolph tie. I note Megan and Hal by the buffet, talking with our department gang. About to stride forth, I halt mid-step, aware that I haven't thought up a story yet. That's interesting. Don't feel the need for one, either. Maybe I can find out what they're talking about and let things flow from there. Scary, but here goes.

When I approach the group, I hear Hal say,

"So Mr. Hopkins brought his wife Dora here to-night." He turns his head as I move in beside him and nods to greet me. "Hi Daryl. Bet you've got a good story on Dora." He hands me a drink and waits expectantly.

Strange. Nothing comes. "Nope. Not really. Except she's a really nice person. Helped Emily find our son a good preschool." Glancing around the group, I see Bernardo and suddenly remember something. "But hey, gang. Did you know that Bernardo here got a promotion?" Everyone turns to look at Bernardo, who lowers his eyes. "Bet he didn't tell you, huh. Unassuming guy that he is. Ol' Hoppy made Bernardo product supervisor yesterday." I raise my glass. "Congratulations, fella. I know you'll do a great job."

Megan and Hilary make exclamatory noises and hug Bernardo. His cheeks grow pink.

I sniff the scent of spicy lasagna wafting from the buffet table. "Think I'll go get myself a plate." I notice that Erin is quite low key, looking kind of white. "Can I get you something?"

Erin's eyes widen. "Why, yes. Thanks, Daryl. I'm not feeling that great." She sits down at a nearby table. "Just some fruit, please."

When I return with our two plates, I sit down beside Erin. "Mmmm," I say. "Great lasagna." I dig in with relish.

Erin picks at her fruit plate.

As I finish the lasagna and green salad, I work on letting the silence be, yet I'm aware of feeling some tension. There's more going on with Erin than just not feeling well. "You okay?" I ask.

She looks at me searchingly. "I'd tell you, but

I'm not sure if you can keep a secret."

After a moment, in which I swallow my pride and tell myself not to get huffy, I nod. "Boy, you're right. That's always been hard for me. Always wanting something zappy to tell everybody."

Erin smiles. "Seems like you're changing, though."

"Think so?" I feel gratified.

"Yep. Think so." Her eyes cloud over. "You've met my daughter Vicki?"

"Why sure. Cute little button. Gorgeous blue eyes. Saw her last week when you brought her into the office."

Erin bites her lip. "I just found out from the elementary school principal today that Vicki's got dyslexia." She twists her napkin. "She's way behind in reading. Turns out she mixes up letters—sees them in reverse or something. They may have to hold her back a grade."

Should I tell her the story of how my nephew has dyslexia and now he's doing so much better? Not sure. God. Please help me be of service here. It won't help to reassure Erin this isn't anything serious. Because it is. Or that she mustn't worry. Because she will.

I find myself patting her hand. "Wow," I say softly. "That's a tough one." And stop.

Erin nods. "It's so hard to see her struggling. She thinks she's stupid." Tears form at the corners of her eyes.

I get some Kleenex from my pocket and hand it to her. "Very hard. You feel so helpless."

Erin nods vigorously and her shoulders shake. She sobs into the Kleenex.

I take a big breath and exhale, resisting the urge to cheer her up. I sit on my hands. And wait.

After a while, Erin blows her nose and wipes her eyes. She lets out a giant sigh. "Daryl. Thanks." A slow smile appears. "I feel better." She stands and picks up her purse. Leaning over, she hugs me.

I feel my shoulders melt. And something like a flow of healing passes between us.

Reader Moment

Interesting, you say. I'm aware of how much more relaxed I feel once Daryl finds his whole Self Compass. This pattern has quite an impact. Is changing this fast realistic?

You've put your finger on it, we say. Daryl is finding his whole Self Compass. Once you find the right path out of a pattern, all it takes is to walk it.

6

TRANSFORMING THE ARGUER PATTERN

A hot-tempered person starts fights
and gets into all kinds of sin.
—Prov 29:22 (NLT)

Geraldo waves over the waiter to his table in the Thai restaurant where he has brought two friends for dinner. Here is what happens from his point of view:

> When the waiter deliberately ignores my signal, I snap my fingers loudly. "Hey. You."
>
> He walks over slowly, just to annoy me.
>
> "Don't pretend you didn't see me." I tap my watch. "Ten minutes. I've been waiting for our entrees ten minutes. I brought my friends here for a great meal and all I'm getting from you is rotten service."
>
> The waiter mumbles something about checking with the kitchen right away and scurries off.
>
> I turn to my friends, shaking my head. "People like that tick me off, but hey, let's don't let him spoil our night out." There is still some red wine left in the bottle. I refill our glasses. Smiling, I raise my glass in a toast. "Here's to good times."

When the waiter hustles over with our entrees, I nod to my friends. "See what I mean? Keep'em on a tight leash or they'll take advantage every time."

Arguer Compass Growth Stretches

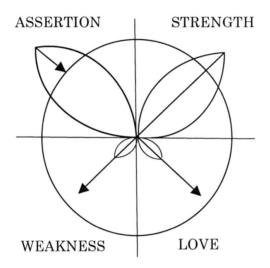

The Arguer and the Self Compass

Stuck on the Assertion compass point with too much anger, you frequently blame or attack others for making you mad. Your interactions with people, even strangers, run the gamut between curt impatience and hostile confrontation, with the odd dose of charm thrown in to disarm them. People around you walk on eggshells. They avoid saying what they really feel, for fear of offending you. You enjoy this power.

What's missing from your personality is empathy from the Weakness compass point and tender caring from the Love compass point. By developing consideration for other's feelings (Weakness), you grow more emotionally sincere. When you exchange chronic anger for nurturance (Love), your aggression is slowly transformed into assertive caring.

You keep the virtue of standing up for yourself (Assertion), but learn to do so tactfully, listening to other people's point of view. And while it's a risk to express empathy and caring, over time the Weakness and Love compass points grace your personality with humble respect for others, and for Christ.

Origins

The Arguer has never developed a sense of basic trust in other people. You may have internalized aggressive treatment during early childhood, then redirected it outward toward others. As a result, you react defensively to any hint of criticism that you perceive is aimed your way.

Or you may have been raised in a home with few limits set on your behavior. When you unconsciously kept pushing the boundaries of civility, no one said, "That's enough!" So you became even more rude and fearless. Nor did you feel guilty about this aggressive behavior.

However you came by the Arguer pattern, you ended up having difficulty feeling close to people. You suspect their motives. Projecting your own antagonism onto others, you believe they're the ones out to get the better of you. You believe people can't be trusted, despite their declarations of good intentions or loyalty. You're easily upset, jealous, and possessive.

Both of your authors have felt the impact of the Arguer pattern. During Dan's early adolescence, bullies frequently beat him up. Dan quickly learned to identify with his aggressors, so much so that he ultimately beat up his best friend. In college he transferred the aggression of his fistfights into constant arguments with anyone who had a different outlook. It took a rendezvous with Jesus to jumpstart his journey into loving others. The Holy Spirit helped him make amends to people he had harmed, recover from his own emotional wounds, and develop a Self Compass that works to this day.

In Kate's case, her Arguer mother often intimidated her with sarcastic remarks and a generally suspicious attitude. Kate developed a Pleaser pattern in a futile attempt to keep her mother from getting angry.

We thank God for what we have learned about outgrowing these patterns. The growth makes it possible to write books together while maintaining emotional intimacy, among other benefits. You can grow, too. With Jesus' help, you can exchange your Arguer pattern for a Christ transformed personality.

Intercepting the Arguer Thought Pattern

Defensive vigilance characterizes the mental life of the Arguer pattern. Your self-talk bristles with frequent thoughts along these lines:

⊕ I can't trust people. They are only out for themselves.

⊕ I must keep testing those around me to see if they're about to turn on me.

⊕ I am self-determining and must not let anyone influence my decisions.

72

⊕ If people seem friendly, they're only trying to manipulate me.

When the Arguer pattern is unchallenged, you are in denial about your harshness. Rather, you see yourself as intelligent and perceptive. You justify being hard-nosed because people need you to keep them in line. You rationalize that it is others who start arguments, who make you mad. As one man said, "I'm proud of how my wife and kids obey me. They know better than to get out of line."

A Pattern Moment

While sitting on his horn in traffic, a man flashes a smile at his buddy and says, "People—I just love to hate 'em!"

Recognizing Resentment

Moving beyond anger-escalating self-talk is no easy undertaking. The first step is realizing that you're angry; then praying for help to calm down. It helps to recognize how destructive your anger is to those around you. Here is Geraldo, discovering this process.

Yesterday I was getting on the freeway from a feeder lane when a red Ferrari came out of nowhere. It zoomed passed me. The guy cut me off only inches from my front fender. *He can't do that to me!* I thought. I stepped on the gas and raced around the Ferrari. I slowed down in front of him and watched in my rearview mirror as he shook his fist at me.

Ha! I showed you. Then I nearly hit the car in

front of me. The guy in the Ferrari took advantage of the moment and accelerated around me. I yelled at him out the car window. "You jerk!"

He roared off. I heard a whimper from the backseat. I glanced back at my two-year-old son. His eyes were wide with fear. He thought I was yelling at him. Not only that, it occurred to me that I could have killed us both.

I took a deep breath, let it out, and felt the adrenaline rush subside. "Lord, help me get over my short fuse," I whispered with new resolve.

Reaching my arm into the backseat, I patted my son's foot. Then I made a point to drive more courteously on the way home.

Transforming Impulsive Anger

Artfully managing anger is an acquired skill. It takes repeated prayer coupled with practical ways for reducing impulsive irritability.

We had the pleasure of leading a young man named Barry into a relationship with Christ. The first few months, he talked a lot of Christ's love. But by the second year, Barry's old Arguer pattern reasserted itself in his personality.

An industrious fellow, by the age of twenty-six, Barry had climbed up his corporation's ladder and established himself as their youngest junior vice president. But his quick-on-the-draw temper, always a problem, grew worse.

"Each time I travel," Barry complained to us, "I get more and more upset. Security people at airports hold me up for no good reason. Restaurant service is lousy. And hotel clerks—forget it! Don't these people know how busy I am?"

One day the president of his corporation called him into the office. "Barry, you are one of the most talented employees we have," the man said. "There's no issue with your competence. It's your temper that has to go. There's a lot of scuttlebutt around the office about how nervous people feel around you. Even your e-mails are caustic. So I'm telling you that if you don't agree to attend ten sessions of anger management training, I'm going to let you go."

Barry was shaken, perhaps more than at any time in his life. He argued that he didn't have problems with anger. That he always treated everyone fairly. But the boss held firm: either the anger management training or get fired. Barry complied, at first reluctantly, but after the first few coaching sessions, his interest grew.

We met Barry several months later at a party. We noticed he was more composed than usual—calmer, actually.

Dan asked how the coaching was coming.

"I've learned a lot about how my behavior affects people," said Barry. "Now I think twice before I say something, or even before I send an e-mail. I try to anticipate how it's going to hit someone. It's working better than the zingers I used to dish out."

"That sounds great," said Kate. "Do you still get upset when you travel?"

Barry smiled. "Last week I got held up with a four-hour flight delay. I bought myself a good book, did a few things on my laptop, and just accepted that these things happen to everyone."

Dan congratulated him.

"There's more," said Barry. "My lifelong road rage has vanished. Last Friday I got held up for an hour on my way into the city. I put on some good music, took a few deep breaths, and kept saying to myself: 'God, help me accept the things I can't change,' and 'Traffic jams are normal. I don't need to upset myself about it.' I passed the whole time without getting mad."

Emotional Life

In order to transform the Arguer pattern, it helps to understand its subtly energizing qualities. You enjoy arguing, for example, because you find it stimulating to hook someone into a good fight. When a relationship is peaceful, you feel bored. When someone expresses love, you grow cynical. If communication flows naturally, you get restless. Afraid of the vulnerability that comes from trusting others, you block your heart to their needs and feelings. Fearful of domination, you watch carefully to ensure that no one gets the better of you. In so doing, you rob yourself of opportunities for intimacy and heart-felt friendship.

Penny is a business executive who came to therapy because her husband of ten years was threatening to leave her. She felt shattered by the prospect of living without him, yet deeply resented his resolve to divorce her.

"I know I've been hard on Mark all these years," Penny said. "But I only blow up when he pushes me too far. How can he take his marriage vows so lightly?" she accused. "If Mark leaves, I'll take him for everything I can get. I'll make his life a living hell."

From Ranting to Respect

A hard fall from a ladder broke Penny's hip and placed her in the hospital. As with many sudden upsets, the serendipitous accident gave Penny an opportunity to face her Arguer pattern.

I still remember those horrid days in the hospital. How I felt so lonely. And angry. I had terrible dreams—nightmares from childhood. My mother lashing out at me with cruel words. My father afraid of her, doing nothing.

How trapped I felt in that hospital room, an unwilling prisoner. One leg was raised in a harness to help set my broken pelvis. I fumed at God and raged at the nurses. I pushed the buzzer constantly. Whatever the nurses did was wrong, and I let them know it.

On my fifth night, a nurse, Margaret, told me that she wasn't afraid of my temper. I recall her next words exactly: "Your words slash people like razorblades." Then she turned and walked out.

I lay there in the dark, speechless, light from the hallway outlining shadows in my room. A creeping realization stole through my body: "I have become my mother."

As I absorbed the horror of this truth, scenes from my adult life flashed in quick succession before me. Dressing down my sister. Telling my father I wanted nothing to do with him. Yelling at Mark that he was a useless, pitiful excuse for a man.

My body coiled with tension. These scenes finally faded away. Then tears. Sorrowful wails. I felt such remorse. Eventually reduced to dry sobs, a plea erupted from my gut. "God, if you're there, please help me."

A deep sleep overtook me that night. Dreamless, and peace-filled. When I awoke early the next morning, Margaret was standing by my bed. "My nightshift's over. But I just wanted to make sure you're okay." She turned to walk away.

"Margaret," I called out. When she looked back, I said, "I'm sorry for how I've treated you." Tears stung my eyes. "You really are a good nurse."

Margaret nodded her thanks and turned to leave.

Guarded Body Language

Fearful of disclosing thoughts or feelings, you guard your facial expressions, preferring a poker face. Your eyes warily scan the environment, making it hard to enjoy what you see. Jaw muscles contract, often leading to temporal mandibular jaw syndrome, or TMJ. Stored-up anger can cause involuntary muscle spasms, which can settle into lower back pain or irritable bowel syndrome. The smooth muscle cells of the circulatory system contract, leading to high blood pressure. You even walk with an edgy stiffness. To anyone who can read body language, the stiffness reveals that your body is a fortress.

Without knowing it, you are resisting the more graceful gait that the Holy Spirit would grant you, if only you'd let go of your propensity for anger.

From "Fight or Flight" to "Stay and Play"

At first it's difficult for the person who thrives on waging and winning arguments to outgrow this pattern, for there is a secondary gain involved. Since anger feels invigorating, it generates powerful sensations of self-importance. Blowing your stack helps you forget your worries for a short while. Adrenaline is a very potent molecule. The rush that comes with anger makes you feel like you can do anything.

When squirted into the bloodstream by the adrenal cortex in the kidneys, adrenaline creates nine instantaneous changes that affect the heartbeat, circulatory system, breathing, and every muscle in the body. This is called the "fight or flight" response. It's like getting ready for battle. Your cheeks flush, muscles gorge with blood, eyes narrow, and you feel an almighty buzz. No wonder so many people like to argue and bluster about.

But the price paid for this adrenaline binge is expensive. As soon as the adrenaline is used up, the body goes into depletion, creating a gnawing restlessness and depression, not to mention spiritual emptiness. Then, too, there is the hell to pay from the havoc wreaked in your relationships.

It takes time to recover from anger addiction. Patience is required to build a "stay and play" connection with people and live without regarding them suspiciously. Your first prayer for Christ's help might feel foolish or naïve. In time, as you persist in this new direction, a spiritual serenity will indwell your body. Many formerly argumentative people who grow spiritually report that they never knew their body could feel so good.

Learning to relax is itself an important step in the transition from arguing to peacemaking. Letting your jaw hang loose, your hands go limp, and your breathing deepen helps your whole body to calm down.

Perception of God

From the perspective of the Arguer pattern, the Lord is a wrathful God, quick to anger and slow to forgive. This perception, however, is in reality a self-statement.

It is actually you, the Arguer, not God, who impatiently metes out verbal and emotional punishment to those with whom you disagree.

Recently we were invited to attend a luncheon with a group of Protestant ministers and Catholic priests. According to our understanding, this was the third in a schedule of ten meetings whose goal was bridging the gap between these two major traditions of the Christian faith. Each month guest speakers made presentations on selected topics. A large Catholic church had been selected for this particular meeting. The bishop of the diocese and the pastor of the largest Protestant church in the city were the two guest speakers.

After lunch, the bishop of the diocese spoke about the Catholic understanding of Christ's atonement for the redemption of humanity. Warm applause showed appreciation for the diplomacy with which he spoke.

Then all eyes turned to the second guest speaker, the Protestant minister. The man marched to the podium, adorned in red tie and black suit with a solemn expression on his face. He adjusted his glasses, firmly grasped a Bible in his right hand, and said, "If you Catholics are finally ready to admit that the Holy Bible is the only authoritative revelation of God to the human race, and if you are prepared right now to receive Jesus Christ as your personal Savior, we have something to talk about. But if you refuse to ask Jesus into your lives, then I don't see any point in staying." When no one raised a hand to accept his offer, he turned on his heel and walked out.

We felt the chill of a silence. It took several minutes for the group to recover. It surely took much longer to heal the emotional wounds the pastor had inflicted.

The pastor was not an evil man, just a man with a skewed Self Compass, stuck in the rut of the Arguer pattern. No doubt he felt he was representing Christ, but he couldn't hide his lack of humility and love.

Since the Arguer pattern has no respect for people's feelings, it makes a point of disparaging alternative views. Yet Scripture cautions: "Whoever says, 'I am in the light,' while hating a brother or sister, is still in the darkness" (1 Jn 2:9).

Reader Moment

I'm beginning to see, you say, how much a person's pattern affects their relationship with God.

Yes. Very much so, we reply. People stuck in the Arguer pattern unconsciously resist the Lord's Love and Weakness compass points, because signs of caring or vulnerability are viewed as naïve and wimpy. The pattern erases the very compass points the Arguer needs from God in order to trust in him and grow.

Practical Growth Stretches

1. Make amends to someone you have judged, abused, or attacked with your anger. Simply say from your heart that you now wish to give up aggression as a major way of coping with life.

Ask if they are able to forgive you. If they are, at that moment, experience the grace of forgiveness. If they're not, give them time. You're still doing your part in promoting healthy change in yourself. They may come around later when they realize you're no longer blowing your stack.

2. Face your emotional isolation and the secret inferiority that caused it. Talk to a friend or professional

counselor about any painful times you experienced while growing up, especially times when you felt humiliated or abused by a family member.

3. Ponder the following Scriptures and give the Holy Spirit permission to help you develop a more honest self-appraisal. Pray for deeper trust in God's love for you.

⊕ Put away from you all bitterness and wrath and anger and wrangling and slander, together with all malice, and be kind to one another, tenderhearted, forgiving one another, as God in Christ has forgiven you (Eph 4:31-32).
⊕ And now a word to you parents. Don't keep on scolding and nagging your children, making them angry and resentful. Rather, bring them up with the loving discipline the Lord himself approves (Eph 6:4 TLB).
⊕ Do all things without murmuring and arguing, so that you may be blameless and innocent, children of God without blemish in the midst of a crooked and perverse generation, in which you shine like stars in the world (Phil 2:14-15).

4. Go to any bookstore and ask the reference person where to find an audio presentation of relaxation techniques. If you belong to a fitness center, try out a massage, or sign up for a Tai Chi or stretching class. If you use relaxation exercises regularly, your body will reach a baseline of relaxation that you have probably never known. Millions of muscle cells will lose their tension. Your breathing will deepen. You will come to feel more at home in your body, wherever you go. Purposeful relaxation is an adult coping skill that provides the

grace you need in moving from anger to love.

5. This week become generous to a fault. Give a gift without needing or expecting repayment. Fulfill a promise joyfully. Send a birthday or a friendship card. Discover the pleasure of being a caring person.

The Arguer Pattern Transformed

It is a year since Penny's accidental fall. She is at home, cooking dinner in the kitchen:

> I hear the front door open. Pulling the frying pan to the edge of the burner, I hurry down the hall, arms outstretched.
>
> "Mark!" When we hug, I feel a ripple of pleasure right down to my toes. "Mmmm," I say. "You feel good."
>
> "Hi, beautiful," Mark says. His hug lingers and he strokes my cheek, then sniffs the air. "Stir fry?"
>
> "Your favorite dish. Shrimp curry." I pause. "Oops." I tear back to the kitchen. The pan is smoking. I resist the impulse to blame Mark for distracting me. Instead, I think, *So what if the shrimp's a little tough. It's not his fault. God, please help me not spoil our evening.*
>
> Mark hums while he makes a tossed salad. I set the dining room table and light some candles.
>
> We sit down and say a prayer. I'm thankful for more than just the food. Mark and I have grown so much closer without my chip-on-the-shoulder ways.
>
> Mark smiles and I feel a tingle in my belly. "Penny, you're a walking miracle. I like how you

don't get upset like you used to."

I beam my thanks. "One day at a time."

Mark gets up and turns on some music. The image of a church basement forms in my head. I was there attending my first Twelve-Step group, soon after my release from the hospital. Since my mom was an alcoholic, I had chosen a meeting for adult children of alcoholics.

Hobbling on crutches, I sat down in the back row. Though irritable from physical pain and fearful that I had lost Mark, I opened my ears and heart to the stories told that evening. I'm sure that God guided me there, because a woman spoke whose story echoed mine. I asked her to be my sponsor. Very slowly, I faced my anger and the fear that drove it. I had to make amends to Mark.

Then another miracle. Someone at our church introduced me to the Self Compass. With it came a guidance system for how and when to use each of my compass points in a balanced way.

"Penny?" asks Mark softly. "How's the music?"

Startled, I turn toward his voice. He's looking quizzical. Then I hear the music. Jazz. Very mellow, relaxing. I lean over and touch his hand. "Just the thing for dinnertime. Thanks, dear."

7
TRANSFORMING THE RULE-BREAKER PATTERN

*Whoever is dishonest in a very little
is dishonest also in much.*
—Jesus (Lk 16:10)

What thoughts go on inside the head of a person in the throes of a Rule-breaker pattern? Picture this young adolescent on a hot summer afternoon.

I aim the slingshot with precision and flick it. I watch the carefully selected stone arc perfectly, as if in slow motion, soaring through the air. Then the sound. Crash. The tinkling of glass from Mrs. Coe's garage window. I scurry away down the alley, chuckling and leaping. Oh, the ecstasy.

Later that afternoon Uncle Zack and I are on the sidewalk outside a convenience store. "Hey, Robbie," he whispers. "Want to learn about the five-finger freebie?"

I nod, breathless.

"Okay. Here's how it works. When we go into the store, go right to a display rack where there's something you want. Pick up a different item and pretend you're examining it carefully.

While you're doing that, grab the item you want with the other hand and slip it in your pocket. Replace the first item and find something real cheap to actually buy, and then take it to the counter."

We enter the convenience store. I stroll over to the toy display. With one hand I pick up a miniature dinosaur and examine it carefully. With the other, I scoop up a yoyo and slip it into my pocket. I stroll over to the counter, select a package of gum, and hand it to the clerk. Buzzing with excitement, I smile appealingly as I pay for the gum.

It's a snap.

Back in the car, Uncle Zack smiles triumphantly when I show him the yoyo. "Thatta boy, Robbie. That's the five-finger freebie."

Rule-breaker Self Compass

Rule-breakers are charming and sociable on the surface, but calculating underneath. Aggressively deceitful, you're stuck on the Assertion compass point. You size up situations according to how you can personally profit by exploiting those around you. There is no sense of remorse.

You have learned to repress the Weakness compass point. You avoid empathy with other people's pain and do not consider your own shortcomings. This lack of healthy weakness results in an undeveloped conscience. Likewise, you repress tenderness from the Love compass point. As with Arguers, you mistrust others, and shun feeling close to anyone, since loyalty and caring would inhibit your need to seduce and exploit.

The Rule-breaker pattern shares with the Arguer pattern a bent toward suspicion, but is more calculating. The Rule-breaker pattern shares with the Boaster pattern a sense of entitlement, but is more aggressive—streetwise, glib, and able to lie convincingly.

Rule-breaker Compass Growth Stretches

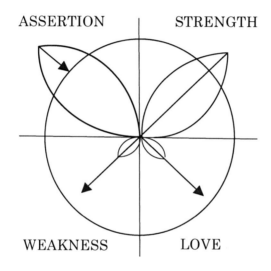

ASSERTION   STRENGTH

WEAKNESS   LOVE

What constitutes growth for someone stuck in the Rule-breaker pattern? You become willing to admit the dishonesty and deceit inherent in this pattern. First you ask for Christ's forgiveness (Weakness compass point). Then you pray for his help to exchange lying for honesty. "If we confess our sins," the apostle John reassures us, "he who is faithful will forgive us our sins and cleanse us from all unrighteousness"(1 Jn 1:9). Once you've done this, you'll begin to experience the warmth of God's love (Love compass point). This love is always there for you, but was blocked by the Rule-breaker pattern. God will help you make amends to those you have harmed, while keeping your dignity. As you find ways to serve (Love compass point) rather than exploit others, the lonely hole inside you will fill with a peace you never knew was possible.

Origins

Young children who experience neglect or abuse have trouble developing an attachment bond. If this persists, some children develop active mistrust in others and conclude that relationships offer more pain than gratification. They abandon the quest for intimacy in favor of manipulating parents and siblings to meet their needs. Often they either model a parent's behavior and/or rebel against what they consider intolerable conditions at home. Usually bright, these children take over control of the family. Mild to severe delinquency can follow, impacting the community at large.

You don't have to habitually break the law to qualify for the Rule-breaker pattern. Milder forms are common during middle and high school years, encouraged when teachers or parents teach children that:

⊕ Winning is everything.
⊕ The most competitive students go the farthest.
⊕ Material acquisition is more important than spiritual values.
⊕ Weaknesses or pain should be covered up.

Milder Forms of the Rule-breaker Pattern

How about the adolescent who steals twenty-dollar bills from her Mom's wallet? The spouse who hides the credit card balances to conceal purchases. The father who makes easy promises to his daughter—and just as easily forgets.

Or this woman in a grocery store:

> I casually walk down the aisle and survey the wire baskets overflowing with candy and chocolate bars. My shopping cart is filled with household items like bread, light bulbs, cereal, and orange juice.
>
> I glance around. No one is in the aisle. With my body blocking the surveillance camera, I grab a Reece's Peanut Butter Cup and stuff it in my purse. As I turn the corner, I furtively tear open the package and thrust one of them into my mouth. By the time I pick up some milk and yoghurt, I've finished the last one and thrown the wrapper in the trash.
>
> Making my way to the checkout counter, I pay for everything but the chocolate and head to the car. I block any potential guilt with this justification: because the chocolate was all gone by the time I checked out, it didn't "count."

Reader Moment

Dishonesty, you say. I see how it creeps all too easily into daily life. One small oversight that grows, like Pinnochio's nose. Didn't Jesus call Satan the Father of lies?

Yes, we think so, we say. Kate looks it up.

Here it is. "When (the devil) lies, he speaks according to his own nature, for he is a liar and the father of lies" (Jn 8:44). Falsehood, it seems, is even more serious a sin than pride.

Rule-breaker Self-Talk

The automatic self-talk of the Rule-breaker pattern focuses on self against the world, and sounds like this:

- ⊕ I need to look out for myself.
- ⊕ It's all right for me to say one thing and do another.
- ⊕ If I don't take advantage of people, someone else will.
- ⊕ Following rules is stupid. Take what you can get and run.
- ⊕ I get a thrill from breaking rules and thumbing my nose at authority.

Pattern Moment

Two men take a break from handball. One says, "I only cheat when it honestly gets me ahead."

Author's Comment: Dan

Dr. S. was an ambitious young psychiatrist with a thriving practice who wanted to share my office space with me. He seemed friendly and professional, so I agreed. I liked his gift of the gab and boisterous, off-the-wall humor.

I really enjoyed the first month of our association. Dr. S. would come bouncing into the clinic, brimming with energy and cracking jokes. But by the third month his happy-go-lucky smile had waned. He came to my office and said that the IRS was giving him problems. Could I pay his portion of the month's rent? He said he'd pay me back the following month.

But he didn't.

"You're first on my list, Danny boy. I'm expecting some checks to arrive any day now from my patients' insurance claims."

But that day never came.

In our seventh month together, Dr. S. asked if he could try out one of the personality assessments that I used with my clients. "I'd like to borrow your computer's scoring code so I can score one test," he said. "I'll pay you for it next week."

Since I was used to trusting professional colleagues, I agreed. So I was shocked when I received a sizeable bill from the testing company. Dr. S. had processed twenty of these pricey tests under my name.

I confronted him.

"I would never do such a thing," Dr. S. protested. "The company has obviously made a mistake. I'll phone them right now and get it straightened out."

He sounded so sincere that I questioned my judgment.

The worst was yet to come. The following week, Dr. S. entered my office, looking crestfallen. "Dan, buddy, I'm real sorry about this, but the insurance companies are hassling me big time. I'm going to have to declare bankruptcy. I'll have to write off the money I owe you." He smiled sorrowfully and walked out.

Finally acknowledging the reality of a Rule-breaker pattern in action, that week I dissolved our association and found a new office.

Dr. S. wrote me a scathing letter. "I'm appalled at your disloyalty. You are not a true friend!"

Emotional Dynamics

The Rule-breaker pattern requires you to deny and conceal your real emotions. Thick-skinned and self-contained, you treat people like pawns in the chess game of life. You avoid sincere communication because you don't want to cultivate intimacy, which could give other people control over you. You suspect those who show you goodwill, believing it to be an attempt to exploit.

The Rule-breaker pattern triggers emotions that stem from social resentment: hostility toward authority, anger when challenged, frustration in the face of delayed gratification, excitement when conning someone, and pleasure when outsmarting people. The price paid for these defensive tactics? Chronic inner emptiness and feelings of alienation from life and God.

Rule-breaker Body Language

It seems like you gaze directly, conveying a fearless nonchalance. You're actually sizing up a person for any signs of trust you can exploit.

How about the soft, seductive look? It beguiles people to feel curious and intrigued. They sense your creative flair, but don't know it will be used against them.

Then there's the innocent smile. This look says, "You can trust me with your deepest secret. I've been around and I can help you out in life. You need someone like me to take care of things."

The apostle Paul understood this pattern: "By smooth talk and glowing words they deceive innocent people" (Rom 16:18 NLT).

From Conning to Caring

Vince stands with his arm around Theresa, holding her close. At the Getty Museum, they gaze at the Picasso in front of them. When Theresa looks up at him with her brown eyes, Vince can't resist. He kisses her.

They turn to leave. Vince glances down the gallery. He freezes. His wife Rhonda is standing there staring, her face blanched white. When Vince's eyes meet hers, Rhonda turns and runs.

Later that night when Vince arrives home, Rhonda has gone. She has left a note. "I'm at my mother's. I will not take your calls, so don't phone me. You've two-timed me one time too many. I'm filing for divorce tomorrow."

"She'll never go through with it," Vince says to himself. "She'll come round. She always has." He sends a bouquet of flowers and an apologetic note to her mother's house.

Saturday morning, he hears a knock on his front door. A man in a blue suit stands there and asks for Vince.

Vince nods. "That's me."

"I'm here to serve your divorce papers from your wife." He hands Vince an envelope, then walks away.

The world suddenly gets very small. It is almost dark when Vince finds himself sitting on the living room sofa, still holding the divorce papers. "But I love her," he yells, flinging the papers across the room. "How dare she do this to me!" Bam! He kicks over the coffee table.

And sits there, numb and silent.

"I really do love her." Panic sweeps over him and he hugs his stomach. "I need her. What am I going to do?"

The Value of Healthy Guilt

To break the grip of the Rule-breaker pattern, it is vital that you learn to feel guilt as appropriate to the situation. Healthy guilt alerts you to the fact that you have exploited someone to your advantage. It tells you that you have used another person as a "thing" and dehumanized yourself in the process.

93

This week, become aware when you are tempted to lie, shirk responsibility, or pull the wool over someone's eyes.

Stop. Pray for God to help you see the situation from that person's point of view. Empathize, letting yourself feel the discomfort of the potential consequences of your behavior.

Reversing roles with someone activates your social conscience. When you trade places with the dog you're about to kick and anticipate the pain and fear you'll inflict, you suddenly have the power not to kick the poor creature. There's an inner shift—not to become a wimpy do-gooder, but to use your power constructively.

Buy a journal and write in it daily. Let your unconscious take you back in time. What are your memories of lying? Cheating? Do you recall feeling some remorse, tinged with excitement? How did the Rule-breaker pattern corrode your life, at the expense of healthy guilt?

You can take comfort that many Biblical characters who came to be highly esteemed were originally Rule-breakers of some note. Jacob cheated his brother out of his birthright. Abraham lied to Pharoah about Sarah being his wife. Miriam hatched a plot against Moses, was struck with leprosy, but after she confessed wrong-doing, she was healed and restored.

The spiritual grace Christ offers meets us all in our trespasses and empowers personality transformation.

Perception of God

Rule-breakers think, "God rewards the clever. God helps those who help themselves." Even for Rule-breakers who pursue a relationship with God, there remains a strong temptation to pillage the coffers and fleece the sheep.

But if you listen for the still, small voice of your spiritual conscience, the Holy Spirit will communicate with you, showing you healthy behaviors and guiding you to build people up, rather than shafting them.

Recall that Jesus requires "truth in the inner parts" (Ps 51:6 NIV). When he declares "I am...the truth (Jn 14:6), this is not an abstract concept, but a costly reality that demanded his death and resurrection. Truth, then, is a quality of action that Christ challenges you to seize. By owning the Rule-breaker pattern, and inviting Christ within, you give his Spirit full reign to destroy what has so long held you hostage.

Practical Growth Stretches

1. Commit yourself to several months of community service work. Volunteer in after-school programs. Help out at the Salvation Army. Pick up litter off the sidewalk. Acts of generosity and service help to counter self-centered thinking and remove the desire to take advantage of others.

2. Read through the following list of Scriptures. In a prayer journal, write your sense of how they apply to you. Record your progress in outgrowing the Rule-breaker pattern.

⊕ We have renounced the shameful things that one hides; we refuse to practice cunning or to falsify God's word; but by the open statement of the truth we commend ourselves to the conscience of everyone in the sight of God (2 Cor 4:2).

⊕ Do not seek your own advantage, but that of the other (1 Cor 10:24).

✠ Putting away falsehood, let all of us speak
the truth to our neighbors, for we are members
of one another (Eph 4:25).

3. Speak to your spouse or a friend about the pain of
your childhood and adolescent years. How you learned
to outsmart people instead of trusting them. How you
learned the pattern of self-aggrandizement instead of
cooperation and love. Ask these people to help you become aware of your Rule-breaker pattern and to support
your growth and change.

Transforming the Rule-breaker Pattern

"So, Adriana," the accountant said over the phone.
"The upshot is that the IRS plans to audit you and Ben."
He cleared his throat. "They're questioning your lack of
reported income for the past two years. Being self-
employed, you'll need to assemble your income records.
The IRS wants to see how these records tally with your
expenses and bank deposits."

"Oh," said Adriana, her heart sinking. *I've got to be
careful what I say here,* she thought. "I'm not sure what
records we've actually kept."

"Well, the bank will have deposit records, even if you
don't. I have an appointment with the IRS in two
weeks."

Adriana hung up the phone and relayed the informa-
tion to her husband, who stared back at her blankly.

Ben paced up and down the den carpet. "What are we
going to do? How are we going to pay the IRS? We've got
no spare cash."

Adriana hunched over in the chair, eyes tearing.

The next day, Ben and Adriana gathered together
their documentation and sent it on to the accountant.

A week later, they sat in the kitchen having coffee. Ben sighed as he took a sip from his steaming mug. "I lied, Adriana. Thought I could out smart them." He looked out the kitchen window at the icy gray day. "I padded my expenses. I underreported income. I didn't declare cash I received. No way was the IRS going to get my hard-earned money."

"Me, too. I did it out of fear. But still, I agreed to it." Adriana touched his hand. "Kind of a relief to get it out in the open."

"Yep."

She frowned. "I forgot to tell you. When the accountant called to confirm he'd got our papers, he said he didn't know whether the IRS had randomly selected us or something had triggered their attention." She looked searchingly at Ben. "I wonder if God is trying to tell us something."

At Ben's suggestion, they got down on their knees and prayed for God's forgiveness.

The morning of the audit arrived.

"Whatever the outcome, Adriana," said Ben, tiredly wiping his brow, "God has done quite the work in us this past week. I believe we're to make more than just a moral decision here. The Lord wants a fundamental shift in the way we handle finances. No more deceit. Only honesty."

That afternoon, the accountant called. "You owe the IRS two thousand dollars. I've arranged it so you can pay by monthly installments if you have to."

On Sunday, when Ben and Adriana attended church, the pastor began his sermon with a verse from Proverbs: "For those whom the Lord loves he corrects."

8

TRANSFORMING THE WORRIER PATTERN

Let not your heart be troubled, neither let it be afraid.
—Jn 14:27 NKJV

In the Book of Exodus, God asks Moses to meet with Pharaoh and demand that the Hebrew slaves be set free.

And Moses' reply to Yahweh? He exclaims, "But I'm not the person for a job like that!" (Ex 3:11 TLB).

God makes several more requests, and Moses responds:

> O Lord, I'm just not a good speaker. I never have been, and I'm not now, even after you have spoken to me.
> I have a speech impediment.
> Lord, please! Send someone else.
> But look, my own people won't even listen to me anymore; how can I expect Pharaoh to? I'm no orator!

Many people think of Moses as one of the strongest personalities in the Bible. But when God initially approaches him, Moses responds in the Worrier pattern: "I can't do it and that's that." Ultimately, though, Moses' meekness becomes the fulcrum for an eventual wholeness and friendship with God.

Like other people stuck on the Weakness compass point, Moses is plagued with self-doubt about his identity. An abandoned Hebrew child who grows up in Pharaoh's palace, he never truly fits in. Is he Egyptian royalty or a Hebrew slave? He ends up ill-at-ease around everybody, as is typical of the Worrier. One day a crisis develops when he observes an Egyptian guard beating an Israelite mud worker. Moses' repressed feelings erupt and he murders the guard, burying the body in the sand. When Pharaoh hears about it, he seeks to kill Moses.

Moses avoids his social troubles as Worriers do—he withdraws to Midian, a desert wilderness where he lives for forty years. He names a son Gershom, meaning "foreigner," for Moses says, "I am a stranger in a foreign land" (Ex 2:22 TLB).

The Self Compass and the Worrier Pattern

The Worrier pattern cuts you off from the Strength compass point. You shrink from the risks required for an actualizing personality in Christ. Disconnected from the Assertion compass point, you avoid standing up for yourself. Not exercising the Love compass point renders you incapable of giving and receiving trust and affection. You end up feeling all alone.

Leveraged out on the Weakness compass point, the Worrier withdraws from social situations, yet longs to participate in life. You lose the virtue of healthy weakness—its humility and empathy—and instead become helpless and held back by procrastination. "I'll do it someday." But that someday never comes.

Worrier Compass Growth Stretches

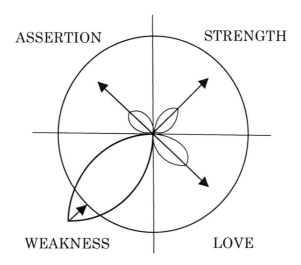

ASSERTION   STRENGTH

WEAKNESS   LOVE

God knew Moses' potential for personality wholeness. After appearing to him in the burning bush, the Lord led him on a journey to make real his potential. Moses did not come around easily, but he cooperated enough to face his Worrier pattern.

Moses kept talking to God, and though he dragged his feet and complained a fair amount, Moses followed God's directives. The result? Moses underwent a gradual but effective personality transformation.

Exodus describes how Moses confronted Pharaoh (Assertion compass point), encouraged people to trust in God (Love compass point), led the Israelites through the Red Sea (Strength compass point), and on Mount Sinai humbly received the Ten Commandments (Weakness compass point).

Slowly, Moses grew into a humbly competent leader, with great compassion for the people he led.

Origins

Children who subsequently adopt the Worrier pattern usually experience loving nurturance from their family of origin. They develop an attachment bond that motivates them toward social contact with others. But then they are often subjected to regular humiliation. They can be criticized for not doing things perfectly by an overly judgmental parent, or may be mocked or shunned for mistakes.

Shauna was pampered for her lovability until the age of six, when she entered school. Her father highly valued academics. When Shauna had difficulty learning to read, her father perceived her as intellectually slow. As an adult caught in the Worrier pattern, Shauna recalled how demolished she felt when her father would call her "Dummy."

Some children are particularly sensitive to criticism from their parents because they are genetically predisposed to shyness. It is normal for such children to pull back for a time, or cry, when faced with new or strange situations. If their parents respond with ridicule or anxiety, it reinforces the children's reserve. And they begin worrying that they are somehow flawed.

Learning theory suggests a "learned helplessness" to explain withdrawn behavior. This can develop by repeated experiences of fearful events over which people perceive they have no control, resulting in a paralysis of the will.

Worrier Thought Pattern

The automatic self-talk of Worriers is frequently self-demeaning, and sounds like this:

- ⊕ If others really knew me, they'd reject me.
- ⊕ No matter how hard I try, nothing works out—I may as well give up.
- ⊕ Dreams and fantasy are better than reality.
- ⊕ No one is as scared and embarrassed as I am.

Pattern Moment

A woman in a diner says to her waitress, "Miss, could you include a couple of hard-luck stories with my chicken salad so I can have a good worry while I'm eating?"

From Negative to Constructive Thoughts

Eric e-mails us, showing beginning signs of progress in changing his Worrier-patterned thoughts:

> I wonder if God is going to leave me stuck like this the rest of my life. Other people are living their lives. It seems like I'm always left far behind. Yes, I know I'm supposed to think positive, but it's hard when I feel so closed up.
>
> But I did go out for a walk today after work. And when I called my girlfriend, I stopped myself from dumping on her about how down I felt. I think the new antidepressant is working too, because this morning I woke up feeling lighter. I actually thanked God for the sunny day.

Emotional Life

Worrier pattern feelings swim in a confusing under-current of sadness, tension, and tentativeness. You long for affection, yet fear rebuff. Since you are so introspective, you're acutely aware of these painful feelings. Yet you refuse to face or discuss them. More often than not, your solution to this turmoil is a self-protective state of numbness.

Another strategy for surviving this discomfort? Fantasy. Worriers often substitute daydreams for direct involvement in life. But fantasies only point out the vast discrepancy between your imagined life and your daily reality.

Loneliness is common. Because your emotions are so blocked, you may redirect the need for self-expression into reading romance novels or writing soul-searching poetry. Lacking close friends or confidants, you may rely on a companion like a pet cat or dog who will not reject you.

Removing My Gray Colored Glasses—Author's Comment: Dan

As a freshman in college, I felt very reserved around people. I had deep-seated fears that others didn't like me. At social gatherings, I arrived late and left early. I felt terrified to raise my hand in classes because my face would turn a brilliant red and my armpits would perspire like crazy. Even worse, my voice would sound hollow and far away. I'd forget what I was going to say next.

If a group of people were talking among themselves, I'd assume they were saying something bad about me or that they'd resent it if I joined them. If several students went for lunch, I assumed they wouldn't want me to tag along.

I remember praying, "God, why do I feel so different from everybody? Why am I so sensitive to the least signs of rejection? Why am I so self-conscious all the time?"

I sought out a college counselor. With stammering lips, I explained my problems. He arranged for me to join a therapy group.

"Would you like to try an experiment, Dan?" the therapist asked during a group session.

"Yes," I said, my palms beginning to sweat.

The therapist invited five other students to form an impromptu group. They warmed up to each other quickly and started an animated conversation. Then the therapist asked me to stand up and approach the group.

I stood up but I couldn't take another step.

The therapist asked the group to freeze the action. They did, standing there motionless like I was.

"What self-talk is going through your head right now, Dan?" asked the therapist.

"They look like they're doing fine without me," I said. "I don't have anything to say. They're bound to reject me."

The therapist asked me to walk among the five people while they were still frozen, and look at each one up close. I did so.

"Dan, what are you noticing?" he asked.

"Well—they look like normal people. And they seem friendly enough. Like they're just talking to each other."

"Congratulations, Dan. You just took off your gray-colored glasses. You're seeing them as normal human beings who'd be as interested in you as they are in each other. I'm going to unfreeze them. I want you to join in with them."

I suddenly realized that my fantasy of rejection was a

distortion in my mind. It was something I could change whenever I decided.

I joined the group, waited for a break in the conversation, and then introduced myself. Within a few minutes I was talking as comfortably as anybody else. The therapist called a halt to the experiment.

When we all sat down, he asked the group members how they perceived me. They shared comments like: "Dan seems like an interesting person," and "He seems a little shy, but he's got a lot to say once he opens up." One girl giggled and said, "I wish he'd ask me for a date!"

That day was a milestone in my development. I had mobilized my Self Compass and moved from unhealthy weakness into a healthy rhythm with Strength and Assertion. I could still feel anxiety but was no longer held back by it.

I felt liberated. I knew that I'd still wear my gray-colored glasses from time to time, but I could recognize them and take them off more frequently. And with God's help, I've done so ever since.

An Uneasy Body

A pervasive sense of unease is observable in the Worrier. In social situations it is common to experience palpitations, sweating, blushing, stomach cramps, or muscle tension. You avoid direct eye contact. When feeling anxious, you shut down by retreating to a corner or beating a hasty exit at the first opportunity. You shrink back from the rhythmic give-and-take of relationships. One man wanted to participate in an adult class at his church. He held back for fear that if he shook hands, others would react with disgust at his sweaty palms.

The speech of the Worrier is often restrained and under-modulated. When people ask you to speak up, it only accentuates your self-consciousness, triggering awkward and irrelevant digressions. Unusually sensitive to the subtleties of other people's voice inflexions and eye movements, you quickly interpret them as derogatory.

Since there is a biological predisposition connected with the Worrier pattern, you may find, in discussion with your physician, that an appropriate antidepressant helps increase your self-confidence and emotional resiliency.

From A Nervous to Relaxed Body

Lindsey has joined an aerobics class in order to develop a more positive body image, and to practice participating in a group (Strength compass point).

I watch through the window until I see the aerobics instructor start her class. Opening the door quietly, I slip into the back row. I'm wearing a leotard, long baggy pants, a size large t-shirt, and a sweat top. All in either gray or black. But I'm there. I mimic the women in the back row as best I can so I won't stand out.

The music actually has a good beat. My feet pretty much keep time. Forget the arms. When things speed up, and the moves get more complicated, I start stumbling. Maybe I should call it quits. This is too hard. But then I notice that a few other people in the back row have lost the rhythm too. Guess I can hang in there.

By the end of the class, I've removed my sweat top. A first. And as I walk to my car, I'm aware that my body feels pretty good. Klutzy, yes. But kind of glowing inside.

Perception of God

Worriers are nervous about a one-to-one encounter with God. "God doesn't really like or love me," you believe. "How could he, when I'm so unattractive, socially awkward, and boring. God requires penance for all the things I've done wrong. I always feel guilty about God, so I try not to get his attention."

But Christ challenges the Worrier attitude in one of his parables. In Matthew 25, Jesus describes how a man departs on a long journey, giving each of three servants responsibility for a sum of money. When the master returns, he rewards the two servants who have increased his investment. But not so for the servant who feared losing the money and buried it in the ground.

> The master was furious. "That's a terrible way to live! It's criminal to live cautiously like that! If you knew I was after the best, why did you do less that the least? The least you could have done would have been to invest the sum with the bankers, where at least I would have gotten a little interest. Take the thousand and give it to the one who risked the most. And get rid of this 'play-it-safe' who won't go out on a limb" (Mt 25 *The Message*).

Through Weakness Comes Strength

While Christ condemns those who pull back from risk-taking, he embraces healthy weakness—humility, not humiliation; empathy, not avoidance. Interestingly, weakness is the only virtue in himself that Jesus ever called to other's attention: "I am gentle and humble in heart" (Mt 11:29).

Indeed, it is through weakness that "strength is made perfect" (2 Cor 12:9). True humility is anchored in both the Weakness and Strength compass points, allowing you to admit mistakes while taking the risks necessary for personality growth in Christ.

Jesus always empathizes with and forgives those who humbly ask. "Anyone who comes to me," Jesus says, "I will never drive away" (Jn 6:37). When you ask him for help, you are mysteriously strengthened. In the process you develop perseverance.

Reader Moment

I find it interesting as well, you say, when Jesus points out that he is humble. Does this mean that Weakness is the most important compass point?

It certainly means that surrendering in Weakness to God is the key to transforming personality patterns. So yes, we think you're onto something.

Practical Growth Stretches

1. Make a conscious decision to outgrow the Worrier pattern. Pray for the Holy Spirit's daily assistance in rooting out negative self-talk and replacing it with compass self-talk. In front of the mirror before you leave home in the morning, try saying:

+ I'm as intelligent as the next person.
+ I have my own unique looks and a life worth living.
+ I may as well press on.
+ Everyone feels scared once in a while.
+ God especially loves a person like me!

2. Decide to actively develop your skills and talents. What are your particular gifts? Find a mentor or join a class to help you develop your strengths.

Active self-development is the opposite of worried withdrawal. If you're athletic, get a coach to work with you. If you're intellectual, sign up for college courses. If you're artistic, join a crafts workshop. If you need help with finances, child-care, or housing, seek out a community agency. Honor whatever cries out for expression within you. Give your fears to Jesus and ask him for help in getting on with life.

3. If you still feel haunted or traumatized by painful events in your past, make an appointment with a clinical or pastoral counselor. Resolve to work through psychological blocks from the past so you can live effectively in the present.

If you have an eating disorder, join Overeaters Anonymous. If you were abused as a child, join a Children of Adult Alcoholics or Incest Survivors group. God will help meet whatever need you bring to a Twelve-Step group. He will heal you as you work the twelve steps and expand your Self Compass.

4. Meditate and write on the following Scriptures. Ask God to help you apply them in your daily life.

 ⊕ The Lord is my light and my salvation; Whom shall I fear? The Lord is the strength of my life; Of whom shall I be afraid? (Ps 27:1 NKJV).
 ⊕ Peace I leave with you, my peace I give to you; not as the world gives do I give to you. Let not your heart be troubled, neither let it be

afraid (Jn 14:27 NKJV).

✦ For God did not give us a spirit of cowardice, but rather a spirit of power and of love and of self-discipline (2 Ti 1:7).

✦ Strive first for the kingdom of God and his righteousness (Mt 6:33).

"You Can Do This"

Kelly parks in front of the school building, turns off the car engine, and notices that her hands are shaking. Here's what happens from inside her:

> Interview time again. How many have there been now? Over four. You'd think I'd be able to land a job teaching kindergarten by now. But no. Not me. Why would anyone want to hire me anyway? I can't even keep control of the kids, let alone teach them anything.
>
> Hold it, now. Take it easy on yourself, Kelly. You're kind and patient with kids. You like them. They like you. Usually. You must go forward here. You're tired of being a nobody to yourself and everybody else.
>
> I pick up my resume package and check my face in the rearview mirror. Pale. Mousy. Limp hair. What a loser. They'll take one look at me and that'll be that.
>
> Okay, Kelly. Where's all this getting you? Right back onto the pity pot. Check the mirror again.
>
> I touch up my lipstick and apply a little blush. My eyes look greener. Not bad. It'll have to do. Gathering up my purse and opening the car door, I say a quiet prayer. "God, please come

with me on this interview. Help me be my best self in you. Amen."

I step toward the red brick building and hear myself say, "Come on now. You can do this."

9

TRANSFORMING THE LONER PATTERN

I will give them one heart, and put a new spirit
within them; I will remove the heart of stone
from their flesh and give them a heart of flesh . . .
then they shall be my people, and I will be their God.
—Ezek 11:19–20

Author's Perspective: Dan

As a salesman for an oil company, my father would leave home Monday morning, return Friday night, and head straight to his den, closing the door behind him. He spent weekends doing what he really wanted to do—still life photography in his den.

On social occasions, Dad rarely smiled or talked to anyone. This was true of his interaction with me as well. When my dad took me to get a haircut, he never said a word and always walked a good five steps in front of me.

One summer morning my mom harangued him into taking me on a hundred-and-twenty mile business trip to Santa Rosa. That trip turned into one endless, lonely day. I waited for him to speak, but he never did. I dogged his footsteps around Santa Rosa as he made business calls. We were together six hours. Not one word passed between us.

Years later, I took a job as a college professor and wrote my first book integrating Christianity and psychology. I autographed the first copy and planned to present it to Dad on a visit to my folks.

Dad sat in his den rocking chair, and glanced up from a book. "Whatcha got?"

I handed him my new book. He looked at the red and gold cover. "That's nice," he said, putting the book on the floor and resuming his reading about photography.

It was only in the last months of his life, when cancer struck, that Dad expressed a feeling to me. Home for Christmas, I asked him about his recent radiation treatments. "I'm scared," he said. "Twice a week they put me into a big contraption where I lie in a narrow tunnel. I get claustrophobic and think I'll go nuts."

When it came time to leave, I drummed up the courage and embraced him in a full-bodied bear hug. "Daddy, I love you!" I said into his ear.

His arms moved slowly to my shoulders. He cradled me awkwardly and whispered, "I love you, too, Danny." He died three weeks later.

The Loner Pattern and the Self Compass

The Loner and Worrier patterns are stuck on the Weakness compass point. Both patterns create distance from other people, but for different reasons. Worriers possess the desire to relate socially, yet are held back by fears of ridicule and rejection. Loners are socially indifferent. They actively withdraw from relationships.

The Loner pattern blocks your experience of the interpersonal satisfactions of life. Cut off from this social gratification, you become aloof and reclusive.

In compass terms, Loners need to take growth stretches into the Love compass point for relational caring, and the Assertion and Strength compass points for self-expression. As you melt the armor around your heart (Love), you learn to recognize feelings. When you express these feelings diplomatically, you become more of a vital presence in other's lives (Assertion and Strength).

Loner Pattern Compass Growth Stretches

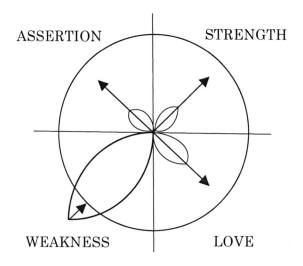

Origins

It is likely that if you are stuck in the Loner pattern, you learned to wall off from others in your childhood. You may have perceived your family as distant and cold. Or you may have identified with an emotionally unresponsive parent who modeled isolation from family members. You formed a weak attachment bond with others, expecting and giving little affection.

While basic physical and educational needs may have been met, you neither experienced nor expressed much liveliness or fun in family life. Consequently, you evolved an emotionally flat way of speaking and a gap in perceiving other's needs and moods. One woman said, "No one talked to me much as a child. I felt invisible, so I got into the habit of watching life go on around me. Eventually I withdrew and quit caring."

Another source of the Loner pattern? A smothering parent that you unconsciously perceived as a threat to your identity. In order to cope with such overwhelming stimulation, you created an inner cave of safety. This hermit-like existence made it difficult to develop social skills and emotional expression.

Children who are developing the Loner pattern pull back from interaction with their peers, preferring to concentrate on hobbies such as computer games or reading. They especially retreat from competitive sports since large motor coordination is awkward. Peer ridicule makes them retreat further into a shell of solitude.

Thought Pattern

The inner thoughts of the Loner disengage you from the stream of life. Such repetitive self-talk sounds like this:

⊕ I can do things better when people aren't around.
⊕ Close relationships are undesirable because they interfere with my freedom.
⊕ If I get to close to people, they will only bother me.
⊕ When people are out of sight, they are out of mind.

 ⊕ I stay safe by keeping an invisible, impenetrable circle around me.

Emotional Life

You prefer to live in a world of your own. Events that provoke joy, anger, or sadness leave you numb. Emotions are blunted no matter what their nature, whether positive or negative, creating an overall sense of apathy, at least where people are concerned.

A friend marries, but you feel no excitement. A parent dies, and you mention it briefly in a matter-of-fact monotone. A child graduates, but you get preoccupied with something and don't make the ceremony.

A young man relayed tearfully that he had been an all-state wrestler in high school. His Loner father never attended a single match. A woman shared her shock and sorrow that her husband didn't come to the hospital for her labor and childbirth. He was busy tinkering in the garage.

Another woman was with her six-week-old infant in the emergency room. She had just revived him from a SIDS (sudden infant death syndrome) episode. Her husband was informed but never showed up. He said it was just too much for him.

Pattern Moment

Two men sit in a sauna after working out together.

One says to the other, "Dad died yesterday. Heart attack. We never got on too well. Not sure how I feel about it."

The other man stands up. "I'm gonna swim some laps now."

Dare to Feel

A feeling is the most private, emotionally-colored part of your perception. You can usually tell a feeling because it's the hardest thing to share. You feel vulnerable and open to rejection. But feel you must, if you want to outgrow the Loner pattern.

Start out by learning to recognize what you are actually feeling in any given moment. Try naming the emotion that you are sensing. Do you feel annoyed? Hurt? Bored? Excited?

Anxious	Angry	Happy	Hopeful
Panicky	Sad	Hurt	Helpless
Bored	Annoyed	Regretful	Relaxed
Envious	Depressed	Tense	Jealous
Cynical	Caring	Confused	Impatient
Joy	Guilty	Excited	Serene

The twenty-four emotions in this table helps to show the dynamic range of human feelings. Try circling the feelings you've had in the past week. Naming a feeling takes it out of the mist of vagueness and represents it in your consciousness for thought and reflection.

The feelings are there within you. But since your Loner pattern has buried feelings even from yourself, it may take some time to ferret them out. Be patient. Invite Christ to help you become aware of what you are feeling. Focus on the sensations that accompany a feeling in order to identify it. Then you can step back for a wider perspective by thinking about what is triggering the feeling. Daily writing in a personal journal will help you unpack what is going on inside you.

Next, try your hand at sharing what you're feeling with someone. Choose someone who strikes you as reliable—a family member or co-worker. Keep it simple. "I appreciated you helping me out today. I felt supported. Thanks." Or, "That annoyed me, when the boss put us down like that."

Yes, it's scary. Vulnerable. But we encourage you to soldier on. You're the only one who can let God help you!

Challenging Isolation

Laurel worked for an engineering firm. She experienced a crisis when her company wanted to promote her to a higher paying job that involved more contact with colleagues. She had sequestered herself for ten years in a little office at the far end of a hallway, where she kept her door shut and attended to business.

Now Laurel was suffering nightly anxiety attacks in anticipation of the increased people contact required for her new position. When she read an article on Compass personality patterns, Laurel recognized herself as a Loner. "I have a choice," she thought. "I can exchange this hollow shell of a life for the one that God intended."

After six months passed, she had made considerable progress in her communication skills and social graces. She made herself go out for lunch with colleagues instead of brown-bagging it. She practiced relaxing her neck and shoulders before returning a phone call. She worked at putting more inflection in her verbal communication. Though it wasn't easy, Laurel turned the promotion into an opportunity for personality growth.

One day an off-hand comment by a co-worker let her know how much she had grown when the person looked her in the eye and said, "Hey, Laurel, you've become a lot more human!"

Body State

The Loner pattern creates a strong disconnect between you and your body. What kind of body language reveals this detachment? Your movements are lethargic, lacking in rhythm or grace. You speak slowly and sometimes barely audibly. You hardly breathe, causing a shortage of oxygenated red blood cells to the brain and musculature. It's like you've created a protective shell, not only between you and the world, but between you and your body. This makes your body tight and numb.

From a Detached to Responsive Body

Marty has decided to try out a massage chair in order to get more in touch with his body.

> I am sitting in the relaxer chair. It's rippling up and down my back. I tense up, gritting my teeth. This is torture. I don't want to relax my body. I like it the way it is. Pulsing movements vibrate through my legs. When will this be over?
>
> I remind myself that I'm doing this because I want to. At least I'm feeling something, negative though it may be.
>
> I sigh. Then I remember to take a deep breath and breathe out to the count of three.
>
> Hmmm. This doesn't feel so bad. The rippling feels kind of okay.
>
> God forbid it should feel good. I smile to myself.
>
> All right. That's enough for today.
>
> When I get up out of the chair and walk away, I'm aware that something's different.
>
> My body is there. With me.

Perception of God

If you are stuck in the Loner pattern, your image of God mirrors your skewed perception of yourself. You assume that God is detached, impersonal, uncaring. "God put the universe in motion but leaves people to themselves," you think, or "God is oblivious to human needs and feelings." The prospect of being touched by God's love is more disconcerting than comforting.

Loners try to avoid church, Bible studies, and prayer groups. If you do attend, it is with marginal commitment. While you draw back from contact with God and people, you may become intrigued by abstract theological arguments or offbeat doctrinal spin-offs. It will take courage to reach out to God emotionally and give him a chance to interact with you.

Jesus eagerly invites you to accept his divine gift of a Spirit-led life in which you will grow "like a well-watered garden, like a spring...whose waters never fail" (Is 58:11). It is Christ's Spirit, the Holy Spirit, who "will guide you into all the truth" (Jn 16:13).

Reader Moment

I'm wondering, you say, how the Holy Spirit actually works within someone's personality?

It's not something we control, is it? we say. Perhaps it's deliberately kept mysterious for that reason. But there's no doubt that, when given the go ahead, "the Spirit assists us in our weaknesses" (Rom 8:26), erasing fear sufficiently to fill the personality with God's living presence. That's a lot of power to enlist, available for the asking, on the journey of becoming one's real self in Christ.

Practical Growth Stretches

1. Practice these affirmations as part of the transforming process:

⊕ I need relationships with people to have a better life.
⊕ I will risk sharing something of myself with others.
⊕ With God's help, I am the only one who can make my life come alive.
⊕ As I participate more in life, I feel my energy level increase and the old fatigue fall away.

2. Practice talking to people. Talk to waiters in restaurant, clerks in stores, the mail carrier, and people at the spa. Keep it simple. "Hi, how are you doing today?" or "Thanks for the great service."
Talk to your spouse and children. Phone your parents or write them a letter. It doesn't matter what you say, as long as you're speaking to someone, making real contact with other human beings.

3. Watch what other people say and how they act in regard to the major events of life. Then deliberately incorporate those same verbal and behavioral cues the next time you face something similar. "I offer you my condolences," or "Congratulations on your new baby."

4. Make amends for being an emotionally absent spouse, parent, or co-worker. Admit how your Loner pattern has affected your relationship with them. Say something like, "I realize that I have a longtime pattern of shutting down and blocking you out. I'm sorry for being this way. I'd like you to help me to change."

5. Ask the Holy Spirit to vitalize your soul and stir your heartfelt potential for life and relationships. Contemplate the following Scriptures, asking God to help you find beauty in your personality.

✦ Ye dry bones, hear the word of the Lord!..." Surely I will cause breath to enter into you, and you shall live. . . Then you shall know that I am the Lord" (Ezek 37:4–6 NKJV).
✦ Let us therefore approach the throne of grace with boldness, so that we may receive mercy and find grace to help in time of need (Heb 4:16).
✦ Confess your sins to one another, and pray for one another, so that you may be healed (Jas 5:16).
✦ Encourage one another and build up each other (1 Thess 5:11).
✦ I give you a new commandment, that you love one another (Jn 13:34).

Transforming the Loner Pattern

Warren was catapulted into looking at himself because his wife of fifteen years told him she was considering a divorce. This distinguished-looking man with a shock of white hair came face-to-face with his lonely life. He relayed that he loved his wife, Patsy, and wanted to make a go of it.

His handshake was limp. He avoided eye contact and spoke in a disjointed monotone. His body was heavily armored with muscle tension, his chest barely moving when he breathed.

During the first month of counseling, Warren couldn't seem to grasp Dan's suggestion that the Loner pattern was the cause of his empty life. In searching for some sort of emotional trauma in childhood that might account for his withdrawal, the image emerged of feeling overwhelmed by his mother.

Warren's mother had invaded his personality and had also overindulged him. A headstrong woman, she had smothered him with too much attention. She never let him develop an identity apart from her.

"I still remember Mom making me practice the violin for hours," he said with gritted teeth. "I felt so bored."

"Can we pray together for God to stir up your old memories so that we can get them out of your system?" Dan asked.

"But I don't want to have feelings," he said. "They're too painful."

"That's only because you were never allowed to express them. They got all bunched up inside and you built a wall of armor to keep them there. But that wall has kept you from being open and loving with your wife and kids."

Something cracked him open as Dan spoke, and some of the armor began to fall away. God was already answering his needs. Warren teared up and said that he felt sorry for all the missed opportunities for intimacy. "I recognize that I've been a fool," he said, "and that I've been the one who has made our marriage a quiet hell."

Over the next several weeks, he recovered many childhood and adolescent memories along with the emotions that accompanied them. One by one, his long-buried feelings of humiliation, anger, and sadness were processed. Each week his face grew more animated and his voice increased in resonance. His breathing deepened and his body began to relax.

By the sixth month of counseling, in a session with Patsy, Warren expressed his deep regrets and committed himself to more fully show his love for her. He still had to work on ways to do that, but the impasse of the Loner pattern was bridged. He was learning how to exchange his hermit existence for the more colorful life of a person aligned with God's purpose.

10

TRANSFORMING THE BOASTER PATTERN

Woe to those who are wise in their own eyes,
And prudent in their own sight!
—Isaiah 5:21 NKJV

Just as the Worrier pattern initially ruled Moses' life, the Boaster pattern held a firm grip on Saul of Tarsus, before Christ transformed him into the apostle Paul.

As a young man, Saul had all the advantages of a prestigious family background and sterling education. In today's terms, he had graduated magna cum laude from Harvard and held a respected position in society. But rather than feeling humble or grateful about his blessings, Saul displayed a haughty pride, indicating that he was stuck on the Strength compass point:

> "I am a good Jew, born in Tarsus in the province of Cilicia, but educated here in Jerusalem under the exacting eye of Rabbi Gamaliel, thoroughly instructed in our religious traditions. And I've always been passionately on God's side...You can ask the Chief Priest or anyone in the High Council to verify this; they all knew me well" (Acts 22:3-5 *The Message*).

If life is like a play, the Boaster wants to write, produce, and assume the leading role. As Paul wrote, "I was so enthusiastic about the traditions of my ancestors that I advanced head and shoulders above my peers in my career" (Gal 1:13-14 *The Message*).

Boaster Pattern Growth Stretches

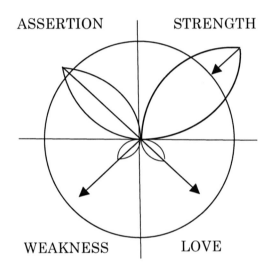

The Boaster Pattern and The Self Compass

If you are stuck in the Boaster pattern, you actively resist the Weakness and Love compass points. You block out admission of faults and genuine caring for people in order to appear extraordinary, both to yourself and others.

The Boaster pattern shares with the Storyteller pattern a need for admiration. But while Storytellers actively solicit attention from others, as a Boaster, you disdain dependency. You employ a nonchalant, coolly superior style for gaining admiration.

While you share the Strength compass point with the Controller pattern in a need to be right about everything, you are less interested in judging other people than in being admired by them.

Jesus was unmoved by Saul's claims to fame, nor was the Lord willing to let Saul grow old stuck in the Boaster pattern. So Christ appeared to Saul as a blinding light and knocked him flat on his face. Saul experienced his first growth step into the Weakness compass point, where he eventually developed humility and empathy for the people he served.

Paul tells the story:

> While I was on my way and approaching Damascus, about noon a great light from heaven suddenly shone about me. I fell to the ground and heard a voice saying to me, 'Saul, Saul, why are you persecuting me?' I answered, 'Who are you, Lord?' Then he said to me, 'I am Jesus of Nazareth whom you are persecuting.'
>
> Now those who were with me saw the light but did not hear the voice of the one who was speaking to me. I asked, 'What am I to do, Lord?'
>
> The Lord said to me, 'Get up and go to Damascus; there you will be told everything that has been assigned to you to do.' Since I could not see because of the brightness of that light, those who were with me took my hand and led me to Damascus (Acts 22:6-11).

The Lord deepened Paul's experience of the Weakness compass point by sending him to the Arabian desert for three years. This allowed Paul time to exchange his Boaster pattern for humble strength and caring assertion.

Only when his personality transformation was well under way did God turn Paul loose on the world. Years later, Paul counseled others on ways to avoid the Boaster trap:

> For by the grace given to me I say to everyone among you not to think of yourself more highly than you ought to think, but to think with sober judgment, each according to the measure of faith that God has assigned (Rom 12:3).
>
> Let nothing be done through selfish ambition or conceit, but in humility regard others as better than yourselves (Phil 2:3).
>
> If we are living now by the Holy Spirit's power, let us follow the Holy Spirit's leading in every part of our lives. Then we won't need to look for honors and popularity, which lead to jealousy and hard feelings (Gal 5:25 TLB).

Origins

While a certain degree of parental praise contributes positively to children's self-esteem, overblown praise inflates it, sowing the seeds of the Boaster pattern. Overindulgence leads children to the conclusion that the universe revolves around them—that the world waits upon their convenience simply because they exist. Parents who unconsciously use their children to impress others make this mistake. Yes, Susie is cute, but there's no need to mention it twenty times a day. Yes, Johnny plays the trombone well, but he is not the best trombonist in the world.

Compass theory suggests that those children who end up favoring the Boaster pattern did not develop a whole Self Compass that allowed them to accept weaknesses as well as strengths. Rather, such children serve to fulfill parental longings for self-glorification through the creation of perfect, brilliant, or beautiful offspring.

Another source of the Boaster pattern is the phenomenon of unparalleled success. Those people who experience a sudden rise to power, fame, or wealth are often adored to excess by their public. They can be seduced into believing the myth of their own greatness.

Thought Pattern

If the Boaster pattern's self-talk were made conscious, it would sound like this:

+ I am superior to others and they should grant me special privileges.
+ I am entitled to admiration and people should feel grateful to have me around.
+ If you love me, you'll do whatever I want, when I want.
+ I have no use for people who don't hold me in high regard.

Emotional Life

The unchecked Boaster pattern creates an emotional tone that is cool and collected. Far from being the result of genuine serenity, this coolness is actually a manifestation of self-absorption and insensitivity to the needs of others.

There is an unconscious expectation that others will do the reaching out, others will take the emotional risks, others will provide the admiration and appreciation that you expect but balk at giving. Why? You are afraid to surrender to caring feelings, equating submission with the loss of power and freedom.

When others are not spellbound by your presence, you can pout by giving the cold shoulder. Secretly, you are troubled by loneliness and a nagging emptiness. You grow especially restless in the face of failure, or if the real world doesn't give you what you believe you deserve. Rather than handling weaknesses through soul-searching, confiding in others, and asking God for help, you rationalize failures and avoid facing your faults.

Toward Consideration of Others

One of the most important shifts in perspective for growth out of the Boaster pattern has to do with actually thinking about the needs and feelings of other people and then taking action that shows this concern.

Here is Emilio choosing to think considerately of his wife:

> I pull on the turtleneck sweater Andrea has bought me. With her watching, I walk closer to the bedroom mirror. The sweater is pale blue. It's too light a shade. She should have known this color washes me out.
>
> I pull off the sweater in silence and happen to notice Andrea's face. Are those tears?
>
> She's hurt.
>
> Okay. I've got to learn to become more sensitive. Let me try something different here.

"Sweetie," I say, turning to face her. "I appreciate you buying me this sweater. It was very thoughtful. I'm just wondering if the pale blue works. What do you think?"

Andrea's eyes widen. "I think this color brings out your eyes. Don't you like it?"

"I like the fit a lot. I think I've got to get used to the color." I don't want to blow it here. What can I say that will help us reach a compromise? "I'm curious. Was the sweater available in any other colors?"

After a moment Andrea nods. "There was a burgundy one I liked, too."

I touch her shoulder. "Would you mind if we go back to the store tomorrow and let me try on that one? Then we can make a final choice."

"Okay. That works."

From Competitive to Cooperative— Author's Comment: Kate

When I began teaching at a new college, I expected to work closely with two colleagues who had established the department.

I had no difficulty jumping into my new responsibilities. Beaming with confidence, I prepared and delivered my classroom lectures and spoke out during departmental meetings, informing my two colleagues of the best way to teach developmental psychology. In casual discussions, I made sure they knew about my depth knowledge of theory in human development.

One day halfway through the semester, my colleagues called a special meeting. They were already sitting at the conference table when I arrived. I was rather surprised that they didn't smile as I sat down, even though I did.

"Kate," said Emily, "Peggy and I need to talk with you about your behavior since you've begun teaching here."

My chin lifted. "Oh?" I asked, eyeing them both.

"Yes," said Emily. "Peggy and I explained when you started here that we work as a team in this department. Decisions are made jointly by all of us. But we find that you are so competitive and self-absorbed that it's impossible for us to work with you."

"Yes," agreed Peggy. "Most of our meeting time is spent with you describing how well your classes are going and how you want things done. I wonder if you care how our input might improve your teaching?"

This was quite shocking. Me, improve my teaching? I glared at Peggy for a moment, then lowered my eyes. Though it was galling, I had to admit some truth in what they were saying. I was too into myself. And lonely. I envied their closeness.

I looked up at them. "No one has ever told me anything like this before."

Emily quietly continued. "We've worked too hard in establishing a good working relationship to have the program marred by someone's self-absorption. You've got a lot of ability. But unless we can all cooperate, it's not going to work."

I cleared my throat. "I guess I've got some learning to do."

I'll never forget how those two women, without argument or rancor, gave me the diplomatic feedback I needed. The department was not going to center on me and I would not be calling all the shots.

With the help of my colleagues, and with daily prayer, I became a team player. I grew to enjoy working with Emily and Peggy instead of competing with them.

No longer seeing myself as being above criticism, I began to compliment them on their areas of greater

134

wisdom. By observing their teaching styles I learned about creative ways to engage students beyond the lecture approach. In surrendering my false pride I came to know the comfort of companionship with my colleagues.

Reader Moment

These two women seem like a godsend, Kate, you say. Can you tell me more about false pride?

They were a godsend, Kate says. I still think of them in appreciation. As for false pride, I'd be glad to explain more. I know a lot about it! Essentially false pride is puffed up, filled with hot air, because it's based on the illusion that I'm flawless, rather than the humble awareness that I'm both fallible as well as gifted with certain strengths.

Body State

The Boaster pattern carries with it a distinctive body language. Chin up. Neck stiff. Eyes searching for the impression made on others.

If you are stuck in the Boaster pattern, you hold back feelings of affection or impulses to reach out to others. This holding back can actually involve developing a band of tension in the heart region. It is any wonder that people can secretly experience you as "hard-hearted?" Instead of transparent communication, you favor calculated self-presentation to ensure that you never look foolish.

Alcohol or drugs can find a place in your life because they enhance your feelings of grandiosity. The Boaster pattern would have it that you are too smart to become addicted. The warm glow of a chemical high can all too easily become a permanent substitute for relating to others with real feelings.

Pattern Moment

A woman is sitting on the examination table, talking to her doctor:

"It only hurts when I swallow my pride."

Perception of God

You typically shy away from intimacy with God for fear that any sign of surrender would compromise your independence. You are secretly afraid God might plan something you won't like. Rather than asking to know and do God's will, you ask God to bless your own will.

Boasters in full bloom see religion as a way to thrive on self-glorification while pretending to serve God. Some brag about their prosperity as a sign of how highly God regards them. There are Boaster leaders who promise to make people rich, if only they will pledge money for big buildings and lavish budgets. Still others expect great dedication and overwork from those who serve them. They have no awareness of the selfishness of this expectation and the burden it presents to others.

Jesus did not take kindly to this approach to spirituality:

"Be wary of false preachers who smile a lot, dripping with practiced sincerity. Chances are they are out to rip you off some way or other. Don't be impressed with charisma; look for character...a genuine leader will never exploit your emotions or your pocketbook" (Mt 7:15-16, *The Message*).

From God Junior to Embracing Christ

Back to the apostle Paul. Later in life, with a fair amount of personality transformation under his belt, we find him reassessing the Boaster pattern:

> You know my pedigree: a legitimate birth, circumcised on the eighth day; an Israelite from the elite tribe of Benjamin; a strict and devout adherent to God's law; a fiery defender of the purity of my religion, even to the point of persecuting Christians; a meticulous observer of everything set down in God's law Book.
>
> The very credentials these people are waving around as something special, I'm tearing up and throwing out with the trash—along with everything else I used to take credit for. And why? Because of Christ. Yes, all the things I once thought were so important are gone from my life.
>
> Compared to the high privilege of knowing Christ Jesus as my Master, firsthand, everything I once thought I had going for me is insignificant—dog dung. I've dumped it all in the trash so that I could embrace Christ and be embraced by him" (Phil 3, *The Message*).

Practical Growth Stretches

1. With the Holy Spirit's help, challenge and change your self-talk on a daily basis:

- ✦ Everyone is special in God's sight.
- ✦ I can feel content being a regular person.
- ✦ I can learn from people's criticisms.

✦ I have a lot to learn about life, God, and myself.

✦ In the Kingdom of God, the greatest is the servant of all.

2. Talk with some friends about how they really perceive you. Be ready to accept what they say instead of denying it. Then tell them that you are tired of being conceited and wrapped up in yourself.

Ask them to help you talk about deeper feelings. Share your anxieties and bouts of depression. Laugh at yourself when you get on your high horse. Find relief from admitting that there is nothing quite so healing as calling yourself on your pretenses, and nothing quite so endearing as revealing your human shortcomings.

3. In your prayer journal, write about how each of these Scriptures is becoming more and more a reality in your daily life.

✦ Jesus says, "I am gentle and humble in heart" (Mt 11:29).

✦ Do nothing from selfish ambition or conceit, but in humility regard others as better than yourselves. Let each of you look not to your own interests, but to the interests of others (Phil 2:3-4).

✦ Christ says, "So the last will be first, and the first will be last" (Mt 20:16).

4. Ask God to help you cultivate a spontaneous altruism. Assist a person who is having car trouble. Take a gift to a new neighbor. Welcome newcomers at your church or social club. Help a college student pay tuition. As you surrender your need for privileged treatment

(Weakness compass point), Christ fills the empty hole inside you with humble satisfaction.

Transforming the Boaster Pattern—
Author's Comment: Dan

I received my Ph.D. in my late twenties, the youngest in the graduating class. I'd read nearly a thousand books and felt proud of my accomplishments. Within the next few years, I published my first two books. While I was wise in my own eyes, in truth, I was a pain to be around.

I was hired as the director of group therapy in a psychiatric ward. I planned to fix everyone—and quickly. I gave lectures to the group to show them how much I knew. I offered advice to show how clever I was. I was the man to save the world.

I'd been there about two months when an older man named Arthur said, "Dr. Montgomery, you've got a big ego that gets in your way."

I was stunned. How dare he analyze me!

A female member of the group asked if they could talk about me for a change.

I was miffed, but I decided to help them out by listening. That day the group came alive for the first time. They exposed in a flash my idealized image of a know-it-all with a Messiah complex.

"You haven't ever shown empathy for my pain," Sally said. "You're so busy impressing us that you're not a real person."

"You need to fix everybody to show us how great you are!" said Arthur.

"Doctor, you need some humility," seconded Sam.

On and on they talked, agreeing with each other's comments and adding to them. I tried to act calm and cool, sometimes defending myself and sometimes listening with disbelief. Finally, I looked at the clock. "It's time to wind up," I said, hoping to shut them up and leave with a shred of dignity.

"Dr. Montgomery," said Sam, "I want to say one last thing."

"Okay, Sam, go ahead," I said.

"For these past two months you've been a jackass."

I left the group feeling shattered. I had entered the room the wise doctor, sent by God to save these people. Now I didn't know who I was. Worse yet, I recognized some truth in what they said. That night I wanted to resign from the hospital and leave the planet. But I decided to pray instead. I poured out my hurt and anger to the Lord. After I'd finished venting, a still, small voice spoke inside me: "Keep going back, Dan. You'll learn a lot."

Reluctantly, I went back to the next group session. I told the people I'd been shaken by what they'd shared. I could hear the pain in my voice. "I'm tired of defending myself," I said. "I'm going to let more of my real self out in this group. Maybe I can learn something, too."

"Thank God!" cried Sally. Then she quit focusing on me and started sharing her pain. I felt empathy toward her for the first time.

What astonished me was that in the weeks to come, we became co-learners in the art of living. My professional input was more tempered with self-disclosures about my flaws and foibles. After several months, Arthur told me that sharing my weaknesses more openly had become my greatest strength.

11
TRANSFORMING THE CONTROLLER PATTERN

Do not judge, so that you may not be judged.
For with the judgment you make you will be judged,
and the measure you give will be the measure you get.
—Jesus (Mt 7:1)

Tanya is a young business woman with a definite agenda to do her job well. Here she is on her way to a meeting.

> Tanya closed the laboratory door behind her and strode down the hall, shifting the heavy briefcase to her right hand as she checked her watch. If she rushed, she should make it to the meeting on time. Good thing she'd got to the lab early.
>
> The briefcase held twenty bound copies of the lab report that Tanya had begun processing at five a.m. that morning.
>
> Tanya frowned. She should have got the report done yesterday. Would have, too, if her lazy secretary hadn't been late back from lunch. So what if it was Barbara's birthday. She should have put business before pleasure.

Backing the car out of her parking space, Tanya drove to the head office. The CEO, Harold Antonelli, would be present at the meeting this morning. She cringed at the memory of their last encounter, replaying it for the hundredth time. She had been standing in line at the company cafeteria about to get a cup of coffee.

"Good morning," came a voice from behind. Tanya turned to see Mr. Antonelli smiling. "You're Tanya Wagner, aren't you?"

"Yes, sir. Good morning."

"Glad to have you on our team. Hear some good things are coming out of your lab."

"Oh," she had stuttered. "Glad to know that."

He saluted a goodbye and walked away.

Such a dimwit she'd been. Talk about inarticulate. What a wasted opportunity to really establish herself as a key player with the big boss. And what did he mean by "some" good things? Had he heard she'd done something not so good? Must have. Otherwise, why had he made that qualification? Maybe he was coming to this meeting to check up on her. Make sure she was pulling her weight.

Tanya pulled up to the gated entrance of the company headquarters. Her car clock showed eight-fifty. Only ten minutes to find the meeting room and get set up. She clenched her fists on the steering wheel.

The gatekeeper signaled for her to roll down the car window. "Your name, miss?"

"Tanya Wagner. I'm here for the nine o'clock meeting."

He scanned a clipboard list. "Hmmm. Your name's not here." He picked up the phone. "Hold on a moment. Let me call up."

What incompetence. How could she not be listed. "I'm in a hurry. Make it fast," she snapped.

After three full minutes, the numbskull let her through the gate.

Tanya wheeled into the nearest parking space, grabbed her briefcase, and tore off toward the front entrance. This was just like the nightmare she'd had for years. The one where she never finds the meeting room.

The Self Compass and The Controller Pattern

Of all the personality patterns, the Controller pattern is the most subtle. Doesn't everyone admire the person who is organized, in charge, and constantly on the go? Doesn't busyness equal success? Who can fault the person who weathers every storm, overcomes every obstacle, and always has the victory?

But there is more to the Controller than meets the eye. The Self Compass offers a clarifying perspective on this pattern.

The Controller pattern is lodged on the Strength compass point, together with the Boaster pattern. These two patterns share a need to be right about everything, but while Boasters look for admiration from others, Controllers judge others as not measuring up to their standards.

The Controller pattern exaggerates a sense of competence. Without humility from the Weakness compass point, you consider any opinion of yours as the right opinion. Other people benefit when you tell them how they should think and act. After all, you're only trying to help them. Unknowingly, you labor under the heavy burden of perfectionism, sometimes called the "tyranny of the shoulds." Even though it's impossible to achieve perfection, you're always striving to do so.

This curse of perfectionism yields bitter fruit. It isolates you and torments others. In the words of Jesus, "They tie up heavy burdens, hard to bear, and lay them on the shoulders of others; but they themselves are unwilling to lift a finger to move them" (Mt 23:4).

Without caring from the Love compass point, the Controller pattern drives out joy, replacing it with a certain dictatorial grimness. It keeps you from nurturing, forgiving, or having much fun.

Controller Pattern Compass Growth Stretches

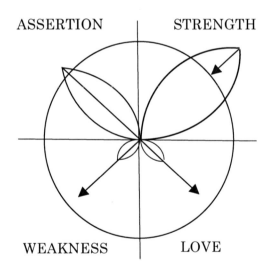

ASSERTION | STRENGTH

WEAKNESS | LOVE

What does it take to grow out of this pattern? Try asking God for help in accepting that you are as human as the next person (Weakness compass point). Express the need for support now and again. Discover how, like Christ, you begin to feel the unforced rhythms of grace in daily life. God can now help you sort out problems previously met with teeth-grinding determination.

Massage the Love compass point by being good to yourself and others. Learn to feel and express appreciation. Get playful. Relax and enjoy the moment. When Love and Weakness are integrated with Strength, you are freed from what one recovering Controller called her "hanging judge." No longer imprisoned by the harsh taskmaster of perfection, you step off the endless treadmill and let God take care of judging the world.

Origins

The budding Controller frequently models a parent's Controller pattern. Parents typically overly train and discipline the child, who becomes the model of adult orderliness and propriety. The upshot is that the child's spontaneity and curiosity is squelched, replaced by overly solemn rule-keeping. "I should never make too much noise." "I should never get dirty." "I should never make a mistake." Instead of playfully interacting with toys and other children, the Controller-in-training is too worried about meeting impossible standards to enjoy the adventure of childhood.

During your growing-up years, it was achievement and perfection that became what made life meaningful. With adulthood comes the unconscious drive to reach a state of flawlessness, so that you'll finally receive the parental approval you missed as a child.

Thought Pattern

These automatic thoughts typify the Controller pattern:

- ⊕ I must always be in control.
- ⊕ I must do everything right at home and at work.
- ⊕ I know what's best. You should do things my way.
- ⊕ People should do better and try harder, and never shrink from duty.
- ⊕ My criticisms are only meant to help people.

The Controller pattern puts the brakes on creativity. Black-and-white thinking dominates—seeing the world in all-or-nothing categories. If you don't find a solution to a problem, it's a catastrophe. If people make mistakes, they're idiots. Thoughts rule feelings, which are trapped in a straightjacket of strict internalized standards.

Opening Up To The Moment

Here is Tanya showing some initial signs of spontaneity.

It was 6 p.m. when Tanya glanced up to see Sean and Tyler passing by her office door. Her briefcase partially filled with materials she planned to take home, she nodded and smiled as they waved goodnight to her.

Her footsteps sounded hollow as she followed Sean and Tyler down the hallway. They were talking animatedly to one another. *I could use some of that,* she thought. *I've had a long hard day. Maybe it's time to take a break.* She sighed. *But they wouldn't be interested in a workaholic like me.*

Sean opened the door of the office building and waited for Tanya to pass through. As she stepped outside, Tyler said, "Say, Tanya, want to join us for coffee? We're going to the Second Cup."

Tanya blinked. "Um. Well, sure. Okay. That would be fine. I'll see you there shortly." She smiled nervously and fumbled to find her car keys, not wanting to be late getting there.

Emotional Life

The Controller pattern keeps a tight reign on emotions. Unduly self-conscious about how you appear to others, you restrain spontaneous expressions of excitement or joy for fear of looking foolish. Openly shared feelings are too uncomfortable. Not understanding or trusting feelings, you judge others who are emotionally open as frivolous or self-indulgent.

If a person corrects you, you resent it. Replaying the scene over and over, you justify yourself and judge the person. Someone stuck in the Controller pattern gets propelled through the day by an inner roto-rooter, creating endless lists, and micromanaging the lives of all involved.

It is common for Controllers to exude confidence, yet suffer from underlying anxiety. Miguel worked long and hard to become a Marine Corps heavyweight-boxing champion. He trained with intense self-discipline and steeled himself to keep feelings out of the ring, not to mention the rest of his life. One night his father flew into town especially to see Miguel fight. Miguel was so anxious to perform perfectly in front of his father that he lost for the first time in his career. A knockout in the first round.

Pattern Moment

A woman is telling her friend about a recent visit to a nutritionist.

"He told me I should eat more fiber and vegetables and cut out red meat."

"Don't listen to that control freak," said her friend. "Let me tell you exactly what you should eat."

Body State

The mind thinks it rules the body.

The body carriage is uptight. Eyes intensely focused. Teeth clenched.

Muscle tension makes it difficult to relax. Typically the shoulders are taut, held several inches higher than needed. A hurried walk reflects the inner need to appear busy and productive. With this level of unconscious muscle strain, it's practically impossible to feel playful and carefree.

Psychosomatic symptoms such as high blood pressure, chronic muscular tension, migraine headache, ulcers, or lower back pain often accompany this pattern. Compulsive overeating is a frequent phenomenon, serving to sedate underlying anxiety, not to mention serving as a secret way for the body to feel some pleasure.

Surrendering the Straightjacket—Author's Comment: Kate

I struggle to get the key in the front door lock, my arms loaded down with groceries and Christmas gifts from Target. No sense taking more than one trip from the car to the condo. One of the grocery sacks drops on the doorstep, some of the contents spilling out. The eggs. My jaw tightens. I forget to breathe. Plunking down all the sacks, I check the egg carton. Six are broken. The family's arriving in an hour and I don't have time for more shopping and what will I do about making devilled eggs?

Never mind. Be flexible. Who will know?

I wrap the gifts for the children and place them under the tree. I check my list. Five things left. I check the time. I'll have to take a quick shower instead of a relaxing bath, but I'll still make it.

The phone rings. It's a friend. Of all times. I tell her I'm expecting company shortly.

"Okay," she says. I hear the quiver.

Slow down, Kate. She's called me because she's in trouble. I sit down on the side of the bed. Lord, please calm me down so I can help her. I breathe in, then exhale. "You sound like you're in pain. What's going on?"

I concentrate on listening and relaxing my body. By the time we hang up, my friend's voice is calm. I sit there for a moment. I feel calm, too.

The doorbell rings.

As I walk to the front door, I realize I'm going to need to ask family members for help. I pray for God to remove my need for perfection so I can relax and have fun with those I'm about to welcome.

Perception of God

The Controller pattern would have you believe that God is more concerned with perfection than with anything else. God therefore views humor and spontaneity as a frivolous waste of time. Self-control is the paramount issue. The Bible or the church should be followed to the letter. Achieving moral perfection and correcting those who err are ways to serve God. Having lost sensitivity to the gentle prompting of the Holy Spirit, you may seek to accomplish worthy goals, yet harm others while doing so.

It is difficult to feel Christ's healing love because you think you have to earn it. But once you're open to a love relationship with Jesus, life takes on the quality of on-going adventure rather than compulsive striving.

Practical Growth Stretches

1. Confess to Christ that you desire a deeper, transforming experience of his love and grace. Ask the Holy Spirit to help you use your self-discipline in a healthy way: make a commitment to express your real feelings in a prayerful dialogue with God. Tell Jesus about what you're afraid of, or why you feel down. If you're feeling more relaxed, let him know. Tell him when you're too hard on yourself, or what a relief it is to know he loves you in spite of your mistakes.

2. When someone criticizes you or tries to give you feedback, don't automatically justify yourself and get huffy. Honestly integrate people's constructive input. Ask for feedback from friends and family: "How do you really see me? Am I overly controlling? Is it true that I'm tense and nitpicky?"

When they give you an honest answer, don't argue. Thank them for their candor. Let them know that you'd like help becoming more playful and loving.

3. As you read these verses, ask God to help you lighten up and find your way to peace of mind.

⊕ If we judged ourselves, we would not be judged (1 Cor 11:31).

⊕ Humble yourselves therefore under the mighty hand of God, so that he may exalt you in due time. Cast all your anxiety upon him, because he cares for you (1 Pet 5:6–7).

⊕ As God chosen one's, holy and beloved, clothe yourselves with compassion, kindness, humility, meekness, and patience. Bear with one another and, if anyone has a complaint against another, forgive each other (Col 3:12-13).

⊕ So let each one give as he purposes in his heart, not grudgingly or of necessity; for God loves a cheerful giver (2 Cor 9:7 NKJV).

4. Do three things that are silly and carefree this week. Swing on a park swing; give someone an African violet; give your spouse a massage; buy a family game and make some popcorn; buy a nontraditional outfit; go to lunch with the gang; take a mental health day to snooze and watch videos. Remember that the best contributions you can make have to do with being warm and accepting of people's differences. And don't worry. You won't lose your efficiency. Now you'll enlist it in a newfound delight of humbly helping others.

Transforming the Controller Pattern

Tanya, several months and many growth stretches later:

Tanya closed the laboratory door and checked her watch.

Five p.m. Pretty good. She was leaving with enough done for today. Tomorrow was tomorrow. It would have its own worries. But there was nothing she could do about them now.

Her secretary was locking up her desk.

"Goodnight, Barbara. Thanks for working through lunch today. Feel free to come in an hour later tomorrow."

Barbara's eyes grew large. "Okay, sure," she said. "Thanks, Tanya."

Pulling out of the parking lot, Tanya's mind replayed the phone conversation earlier today with Mr. Antonelli.

"I want to thank you for a job well done on that grant proposal, Tanya. Got us the funding we needed for that new research."

"Glad to hear it, sir."

"You know, everyone else calls me Harold. I'd be pleased if you did too."

"Oh. Certainly, sir, er, Harold. Be glad to."

Tanya shifted uncomfortably in her car and hunched her shoulders over the steering wheel. How could she have responded so awkwardly. She should have noticed how everyone else called him Harold. And calling him sir again, just after he'd asked her to call him Harold. Tanya grimaced.

Hold on here. She was shoulding again.

She kept doing this to herself. Why couldn't she just stop it? Would she ever get this right?

Wait a minute. She had to remember that this pattern was way too strong to fight by herself. "Dear Jesus," Tanya whispered, "Please help me. Remove my judgmental thoughts. Clear them right out of my head. Help me see your take on things, not mine. Thank you. Amen."

At the intersection, the stoplight turned red. As Tanya waited for it to turn green, she felt the release of tension. A peace crept through her chest and permeated her body. Tanya glanced out the window. That was a neat looking park. She'd have to take a walk there this weekend. But now she had to get to La Scala.

Grateful to find nearby parking, Tanya grabbed a wrapped gift from the backseat and headed to the front door of the restaurant. She entered and peered around the softly lit dining room, seeing candles flickering on tables and in wall sconces. Crystal stemware gleamed on white tablecloths. How attractive this place was. How many times had she been here and never noticed?

But she was noticing now.

She walked up to a round table for eight where five people were already seated. Her officemates rose to greet her.

"Is Barbara on her way?" asked Mike.

Tanya nodded. "Yep. Her boyfriend is picking her up from work. Said he'd bring her right here."

A few minutes later, Barbara appeared at the restaurant entrance. As she walked toward their table, Tanya and her officemates call out, "Surprise!"

Mike brought out a stash of balloons from under the table. "It's a wedding shower!" he shouted.

Barbara hugged everyone, laughing in delight.

Tanya sat back in her chair, satisfaction welling up within her.

I planned this well overall, she thought.

I'm letting go of the fact that I forgot Barbara's card.

And that the waiter spilled water on my skirt.

Reader Moment

I'm seeing the fluidity in Tanya, you say. That she's drawing from her whole Self Compass to feel this relaxed, yet still has confidence.

Exactly, we say. She's flowing with life more, and relaxing about what she can't control.

I'm wondering, though, you continue, if you have any tips for dealing with people when their patterns are in full sway?

Very important, we say. And coming up. Right after we have a look at common pattern combinations.

12
UNDERSTANDING PATTERN COMBINATIONS

(Jesus Christ) will make us beautiful and whole
with the same powerful skill by which he is
putting everything as it should be.
—Phil 3:21 *The Message*

It is normal to discover that you are in the grip of more than one personality pattern. To be stuck in one pattern with your spouse, and another with people at work, for example. What are some common combinations and what can be done about them?

The Pleaser and Controller patterns are frequently combined. Feeling compelled to make everyone perfectly happy, you rush about accomplishing things for others with great efficiency, but feel hurt and secretly judge them when they take you for granted.

Here's another possible combination: The Loner and Boaster patterns. You prefer time spent alone to develop what you perceive as considerable creative talent. When pushed for more overt emotional expression, you react coolly, surprised that anyone would be so bold as to criticize you.

Or what about the Arguer and Loner pattern combination? You keep emotional distance from others, but when they press in for more companionship, you erupt with an angry outburst to keep them at bay. You with an angry outburst to keep them at bay. You immediately pull back into your hermit-like shell to protect yourself from the consequences of such intense emotion.

Then there is the Arguer and Storyteller pattern combination. You tell stories meant to capture people's attention and evaluate your social life according to how much attention you receive. You take it personally if someone ignores you and later explode into a fury of hurt indignation, telling all to someone unconnected to this awful experience exactly what you endured.

How does the Boaster and Worrier pattern combination function? You feel lonely most of the time and long for more interaction with people. But when you do get involved, perhaps in a group activity, the condescending attitude of the Boaster pattern kicks in. You inwardly evaluate everyone in the group less talented than you. And feel justified in retreating back to your static state of superior loneliness.

Top Dogs and Underdogs

It is common for individuals to favor either the upper or lower halves of the Self Compass. That is, you overuse Strength and Assertion, making you a top dog; or you overly rely upon Love and Weakness, making you an underdog. Top dogs strive to control people through intimidating and criticizing. Underdogs control others through pleasing and withdrawing.

Top Dog Pattern Combination

The top dog pattern combination mixes exploitive aggression with judgmental control. You get annoyed at practically anything that inconveniences you. Breaking a few rules to rectify that inconvenience is not a problem. And you don't mind critically attacking the person responsible for this inconvenience who made you mad in the first place. If anyone dares to criticize you, you justify your point of view with defensive, stubborn pride.

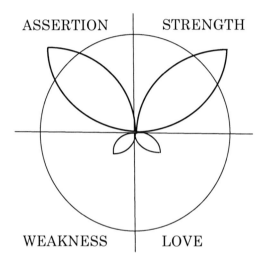

ASSERTION   STRENGTH

WEAKNESS   LOVE

Top Dog Pattern Combination

Underdog Pattern Combination

The underdog pattern combination swings between melodramatic pleasing and avoidant helplessness. You attempt to please and charm people with stories that are inconsequential and boring. You long for close relationships, but only achieve surface level interactions. Because you avoid risking an honest expression of how you feel, or actions you might take to develop your own identity, you stay stuck in secret depression and loneliness.

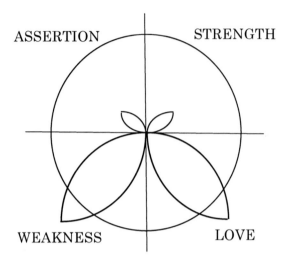

ASSERTION   STRENGTH

WEAKNESS   LOVE

Underdog Pattern Combination

Author's Comment: Kate

The Controller, Boaster, and Pleaser are the particular pattern combinations I've had to face: the Controller and Boaster patterns at work, and the Pleaser and Controller patterns at home. It was much easier to deal with my patterns at work than at home, since work relationships are less intense, less emotional.

I've pretty much outgrown the Boaster pattern with plenty of prayer and the willingness to admit and release my entitled attitude. The Pleaser pattern has receded as well, though occasionally I get caught up in family stress and try to perfectly please my children. My sense of serenity evaporates when I let other people determine how I feel. With both Christ's help and Dan's, I regroup and frequently find the inner peace that passes understanding.

158

The Controller pattern is the one I've found the most resistant to change. I catch myself thinking judgmental thoughts, particularly about Dan—little things like forgetting to signal when he's driving. I blow them out of proportion with my disapproving attitude. The good news is that I typically pray for help to keep my mouth shut, as well as for release from those harm-filled thoughts. If I do get snippy, I make a quick and heartfelt apology, because I now understand how it hurts Dan. But there is no question that I need to surrender this pattern to God on a daily basis.

Author's Comment: Dan

The several patterns that I've discussed in this book I think I have outgrown with God's guidance. But there are certainly other pattern combinations I've struggled with at varying times in my life. In my early twenties, for example, God helped me become aware of the stoic, over-controlled nature of my relationship with him. The "go-it-alone" attitude of the Loner pattern and perfectionist outlook of the Controller pattern kept me from feeling God's love. Striving to be the best Christian I could left a hollow feeling inside me, because I was always thinking about God without really knowing how to emotionally surrender to him.

A major way that I gradually outgrew the Loner and Controller patterns was through feeling the Holy Spirit as a comforting presence in my body. Then, following the Spirit's counsel, I started sharing more of my emotional life with the people around me. And sure enough, these relationships came alive.

In fact, for a few years, I overdid my emotional openness and got stuck in the Pleaser pattern, always trying to love everyone. Again the Holy Spirit counseled me, this time to develop more assertion so I'd have a more balanced Self Compass to interact with God and people.

Action Steps

To determine which pattern combinations are at work in your life, ask yourself which of the eight patterns seem most like you. Check it out with people whom you know and trust. Ask them to read one or two of the chapters on the eight patterns and see if any of it reminds them of you. Completing *The Self Compass Inventory* in Chapter Three will offer important insights.

If you register more than one pattern, begin with the one with the highest score—the one that is harming you and others the most. Re-read the chapter on that particular pattern. Treat the growth stretches as vital in expanding your personality, yet pray for wisdom in balancing your self-determination with God's grace. You're after discipline combined with surrender: the Strength and Assertion, Love and Weakness compass points in rhythmic harmony. Don't worry. Christ's own resourcefulness will help to heal and guide you.

Reader Moment

I think I'm getting the hang of this.

And you're going to discuss how to counter these patterns, right?

Yes, indeed. Coming up next, in Part III.

Part III
COMPASS LIVING

This is to my Father's glory, that you bear much fruit,
showing yourselves to be my disciples.
—Jesus, Jn 15:8 NIV

It takes considerable courage to face and begin dismantling the personality patterns of a lifetime. Part III provides further ways to apply the wisdom of the Self Compass in your daily life.

To start, we address healthy ways to handle other people's patterns at home and at work.

We end with a chapter on the virtues embedded in the Self Compass; virtues that are present in every pattern, but take actualizing the LAWS of personality to bear fruit.

You can now reap the benefits of these virtues, like good cheer and creativity, empathy and discipline, from surrendering these patterns to the Holy Spirit's transforming power, "for all of us, with unveiled faces, seeing the glory of the Lord as though reflected in a mirror, are being transformed into the same image from one degree of glory to another" (2 Cor 3:18).

13
COUNTERING OTHER PEOPLE'S PATTERNS

Watch, stand fast in the faith, be brave, be strong.
Let all that you do be done with love.
—1 Cor 16:13 NKJV

It is a hard, clear blue sky this afternoon in Judea when Jesus speaks. The crowds come. And come, from villages all around. They press in. Pushing closer, to hear his words. His disciples with him, Jesus preaches, his voice penetrating the desert air, reaching the hearts open to his word.

But someone interrupts him, to say that his family has arrived. They wish to speak with him, but are unable to get through the densely packed crowds to his side.

Jesus' response is scandalous. He says his family are those all about him, not limited by birth. He refuses to let his family presume upon him and his mission (Mt 12:46-50).

Here is assertion, as Jesus stands against an attempt to manipulate by the Controller pattern. And here is a primary principle: conform not to other people's patterns, Jesus says, but to God's way for living life.

How? you ask.

How do you stand against other people's patterns without succumbing to pattern manipulation yourself?

Challenging, we agree.

Our recommendation? Employing the power of a whole Self Compass. To that end, here are some strategies that utilize the LAWS of personality health for neutralizing the impact of these patterns.

Dealing with the Pleaser Pattern

Janice is married to Greg, who is learning how to counter the effects of her Pleaser pattern. She is motivated to change, and has agreed that Greg can address this with her tactfully.

Greg is with Janice as she ends a phone conversation with their grown son, David:

> "Of course, dear. I'd be glad to baby-sit for you. You both need a break when you're looking after two little children."
>
> Janice hangs up the phone and turns to Greg.
>
> "I hope you don't mind, dear, but I just agreed to baby-sit next weekend for David and Sharon. David said they really need a break."
>
> Greg looks at her, concerned. "Guess you didn't remember that we have plans for a getaway next weekend." (Notice how Greg keeps his cool, explains the problem, and lets Janice feel the tension.)
>
> Janice's hand goes to her mouth. "Oh, that's right. Oh, I'm so sorry. I forgot. I heard the stress in David's voice and I just couldn't say no."

164

"Okay. What about calling him back and telling him what you just told me? You could baby-sit the following weekend."

Janice leans forward. "Oh my, I just don't know. I hate to disappoint them. They're having a hard time of it lately. I worry that their marriage won't stand the stress. Could we change our plans for the following weekend?"

Greg frowns. "Whoa. This doesn't feel good to me. You're placing our relationship a definite second here because of your need to please David. That hurts."

Janice winces. "I'm so sorry, Greg."

Greg stops himself from reassuring her that it's okay. "I agree that David and Sharon need a break. But they don't even know about our plans." Greg looks at her and says softly, "It's your choice, Janice."

(Greg uses the Strength compass point to keep from rescuing her and the Love compass point to reach out to her.)

Janice tears up and reaches for a tissue. "I need to think and pray about this for a little while," she murmurs. She heads to the bedroom. Ten minutes later she emerges, a look of relief in her eyes.

Janice smiles as she sits down by Greg. "I just called David and told him about our plans. I'm going to baby-sit the following weekend so you and I can have our date." She puts her arms around him. "Thanks for your honesty, honey."

Greg expresses his feelings with caring assertion and holds with his point of view even though he knows that it will be uncomfortable for Janice to hear. Nor does Greg take over for Janice. He gives her the opportunity to take responsibility for her actions.

This allows Janice to assert herself and demonstrate that she shares his priority of placing their marriage first.

Living with the Storyteller Pattern

The Storyteller patterned person wants your total attention as long as you're willing to give it. How do you interrupt a steady stream of non-stop talking? By practicing some polite conversation stoppers.

A touch on the arm, and, "Paula, I'm feeling overloaded right now. You're giving me so many details that I lose track of what you're really saying."

Or, "I'm glad you had a good time at the party, Ryan. I need to get back to work." Stand up and walk away, with a polite "See you later."

Agree that something is indeed exciting, then ask, "Would you be interested in hearing something I have to say?"

Watch for a phrase or topic that triggers something you want to talk about and then step in to forcefully change the subject. You're not being rude, just shifting the person's monologue into a dialogue.

When you consistently give into the onslaught of storytelling, inner resentment can make you miserable, helping neither you nor the person caught in the Storyteller pattern.

If someone with the Storyteller pattern negatively impacts your life, use caring assertion to say when you've had enough. Make sure you get time alone to recover. Refer them to this book, if they seek help. Suggest prayer and pastoral counseling. If you're willing to support them in their growth, discuss how that might work. These principles apply to countering any of the personality patterns.

Here is Carmen dealing with her boyfriend Boone's Storyteller pattern. They have met after work and Boone is in full swing:

> "So anyway, I just had the best time at the gym. They just redecorated the whole place. I don't know if you've been recently but I was so surprised to see the new carpeting and they've totally repainted the men's locker room. Say, did I tell you I had lunch with Ernesto? I met him in the men's locker room, see, and we discovered that we both really like to play pool. There's this cool place he knows about that I've never been to, but I'd love to take you sometime. How about tonight? Want to try it out? I can teach you the basic strokes. It'd be fun, huh, Carmen? Anyway, I found out how to..."
>
> Carmen touches Boone on his arm and waits until he stops talking and gives her eye contact.
>
> "Boone." She smiles as she sighs. "I got overwhelmed with all that you just told me. I think I took in that the gym's been redecorated, but I lost you after that." Carmen takes his hand. "Can you tell me just one short thing you really want to get across to me and leave it at that?"
>
> Boone looks down. "I know I get too excited sometimes. It's just that..." He bites his lip. "Okay. Here goes. One thing. Would you like to play pool with me tonight?"
>
> Carmen grins and hugs him. "I'd love to."

Living with the Arguer Pattern

The Arguer pattern attempts to coerce compliance through instilling fear. Arguers want you to placate their anger, respond submissively to their wishes, and feel insecure around them.

When the Arguer pattern is allowed full reign, these manipulations work. People kowtow to Arguers, scared to confront them because they don't know how to diffuse the pattern's intimidating power.

Work on pulling back from any anger directed your way; you'll feel less fear. Avoid arguing back. Their anger is not about you—it's about their pattern. You don't need to feel put on the spot or pressured by their demands. In fact, you don't need to do a thing that they command.

Pray for inner calm and for God to give you the right words or actions. Picture the whole Self Compass and place yourself in the middle of it as you call on the Lord for help and protection. Say to yourself, "I can stick to my point of view. I can do what I need to do."

Speak to them in a monotone devoid of emotion so they can't use your feelings against you or even read your true feelings. If you feel that the situation is escalating in spite of your impartial input, quietly remove yourself from the situation. Get up and say that you've got to go. That you'll talk later when things have calmed down. Or hang up the phone after you say a quick goodbye.

And of course, whether at home or at work, if the situation becomes abusive, get advice and help from your pastor, human resources department, or at the law enforcement level.

Here is Norm beginning to get the idea of how to interact at work with his Arguer patterned boss, Bruce.

"Norm," yells Bruce from his office, "did you make that call to Zeropoint?"

Norm gets up from his desk and walks to the office doorway. "Did you ask me something, sir?"

Bruce slams his pen down on the desk. "Of course I asked you something. Are you wearing earplugs? Did you call Zeropoint?"

"Yes, I did."

"Well? Did you get the sale, or what? Why do I have to pull it out of you?"

Norm points to a report on the top of Bruce's in-file and replies calmly, working on breathing deeply. "I made the Zeropoint sale. The details are in my report that I put on your desk at ten o'clock this morning."

Bruce blinks. "Oh. Well." He picks up the report and glances at the first page. With a brief nod, he stands up and puts out his hand. "Hey, not bad, Norm." Bruce smiles as Norm turns to leave. "Not quite the profit margin I'd hoped for, but not bad at all."

Norm ignores the comment, returns to his desk, and resolves to reconsider a job offer from Zeropoint made to him by the CEO the day before.

Handling the Rule-breaker Pattern

Rule-breakers search out naïve, gullible targets and use their charm for ulterior motives. Pleaser patterned people are particularly at risk because a lack of the Assertion compass point prevents their ability to discern someone's true intent. The best defense against this pattern is to understand what motivates the Rule-breaker: the thrill of deception for personal gain. Rule-breakers feel proud of their ability to work the system undetected or to get what they want from a relationship without giving back.

One way to handle the Rule-breaker pattern is to state clearly your refusal to go along with a plan you perceive as dishonest. If your teenager has a pattern of lying, for example, you practice resisting a glib apology or a fervent promise of new behavior.

Once you become aware that there is a discrepancy between what someone says and actually does, it's important to do something about it. You want to make it not pay for them to engage in con artist behavior at your expense. They learn that you don't just let it go. Keep your cool while using the Assertion and Strength compass points. Anger and disdain only empowers the Rule-breaker.

Jim decides to call up his friend Sam on his cell phone:

"Sam, about this concert you want me to get tickets for and that you'll pay me back? I've changed my mind. I'm going to let you go ahead and get the tickets. I don't feel comfortable getting them because the last time this happened and I got the tickets, I never got paid back." (Notice how the use of "I" instead of "You" statements avoids aggressive blaming. The emphasis is on a decision made, clearly and briefly explained.)

"Hey, buddy, that was just an oversight on my part. You go ahead and get those tickets, huh? My boss has got me so busy and we sure want to get good seats..."

"Nope. What I said still stands, Sam. Talk to you later. Bye." (Jim sticks to his main point and removes himself from further attempts to manipulate him.)

Such monitoring and accountability keeps you from being hurt by a Rule-breaker and keeps them on a straighter path in their relationship with you.

Responding to the Worrier Pattern

Jane is talking in the church kitchen with Eric after choir practice. Both are volunteer librarians for the large church choir. Aware of Eric's Worrier pattern, Jane wants to interact with him authentically, using her whole Self Compass. Praying for God's help in the conversation, she reminds herself that it is Eric's choice as to how he responds.

"I'm so useless," says Eric, head hung low. "Can't get a job no matter what I do. No one would want to hire me anyway."

"I wouldn't say that's true," Jane replies calmly. "You've made it to the finals selection twice, haven't you? And you've got a lot of job skills to offer in the computer world."

"Oh, you're just saying that to be kind." Eric shakes his head. "It's getting so I might as well not bother applying. Not worth the effort." He looks down at the floor.

Jane waits until Eric looks at her. "Eric, I'm wondering what you would like from me right now."

Eric shrugs his shoulders.

Jane sips her coffee.

"I don't know." Eric sighs. "Nobody under-stands me."

"I'd like to be your friend, Eric. How do you think I can do that?"

Eric bites his lip, but then lifts his head to make eye contact. "I, uh, I like that you listen to me," he says. "That you don't get mad."

"I appreciate you telling me that, Eric." Jane nods gently. "And I like how you made me tea last week when I felt down about my son."

Eric smiles shyly, then says, "Glad that helped."

Unwilling to let the Worrier pattern prevail by re-sponding impatiently, Jane kept both of their dignities in tact with her assertive caring. She used the LAWS of her Self Compass for balanced, honest communication.

Jane will do well if she can remember that it is not her job to make Eric's life work out. When he expresses self-loathing or makes deflating remarks about his inep-titude, she can listen for about two minutes and then change the topic or close the conversation so that she can turn to other pursuits. This kind of patience com-bined with firmness may help Eric shift his perspective now and then without dragging them both into a slough of despond.

The key to anyone's success in countering this pat-tern is to let the person do their own failing with occasional objective feedback thrown in. Don't feel overly sad, mad, or sorry for them. If you do get hooked by these powerful feelings, get it off your chest with someone else so you can stop worrying about their wor-ries and get on with your life.

Working With the Loner Pattern

Debbie and Chuck work for the same T-shirt company. This particular morning, Debbie comes into Chuck's office, smiling happily.

"So Chuck, how do you like my new line of sweatshirts?" asks Debbie. She holds up a bright orange sweatshirt in front of her. It's stenciled with gold lamé letters and reads: "Go Tigers!"

Chuck looks up from reading a report and gazes at it for a moment, his face expressionless. "Don't like it."

Debbie's eyebrows pucker. "How come? What's the matter with it?"

Chuck shrugs. "Just don't like it. Bit bright, I guess." He returns to reading his report.

Debbie stands there for a moment, ready to turn on her heel and stomp out. But she decides to stay put. Sitting down in the chair in front of Chuck's desk, she waits.

After a few moments, Chuck glances up from the report. "Need something else?"

"Chuck, is there anything you do like about this sweatshirt?" She hands it over to him.

He takes it and rubs a finger over the sleeve. "The material," he says. "It's soft. Cushy." He hands it back to her.

"How do you think the design could be improved?"

Chuck looks up at the ceiling. "Well, you could darken the orange. And change the lamé to appeal more to men." He glances out the window.

"Hey, thanks, Chuck. Helpful input."

With a slight smile, he briefly meets her eyes. "No problem."

Debbie bounces out of his office with a friendly wave.

Debbie is choosing not to frustrate herself unnecessarily about Chuck's restrained style of communication. She accepts that someone stuck in a Loner pattern is not gregarious. Accordingly, she slows down the pace of the interaction, gives him time to respond, and appreciates what she does get from Chuck in the exchange, which, though minimally expressive, is nonetheless thoughtful and objective. Debbie has reframed her expectations so that she is satisfied when Chuck meets her request for input. She knows to choose someone else if she needs an emotionally stimulating dialogue.

If you are married to a Loner, keep in mind that shows of impatience and anger only serve to increase the emotional distance you experience, because the Loner pattern pulls back even further from such intensity. Instead, call on God's help for patience and kindness, calmly stating your need and making reasonable suggestions about how your partner can meet it.

Living with the Boaster Pattern

The Boaster pattern requires fawning admiration from others. But while you initially appreciate many captivating qualities, it is difficult to sustain a relationship as the footlight to the Boaster pattern's spotlight. A sense of entitlement creates a barrier between Boasters and those who desire a closer relationship. And Boasters frequently react to criticism by withdrawing what little attention they do give to others.

So how do you counter the Boaster pattern using the LAWS of the Self Compass?

Catch them being kind. Honestly compliment them when they do something considerate of you. Tell them what it means to you. "I really appreciate how you picked up my dry cleaning today. That was so thoughtful. It feels like you're thinking about me during the day, even though we're apart."

Diplomatically speak out if there is something you think needs addressing, but avoid nagging or critical remarks. Let's say you're out to dinner with your friend, Mary Lynn:

"Can I check something out with you?"
"Sure."
"I know you got held up at work, so you were late meeting me for dinner, but I'm wondering what kept you from calling me."
"Oh. Yes. I got so absorbed in the mix-up at work, it went right out of my mind. Glad to have gotten here at all."
"So you don't think a phone call would have helped me out?"
"Well, yes. Of course it would. Sorry I didn't call."
"Thanks. Apology accepted. Mary Lynn, I appreciate you understanding that something like this can hurt unless it gets cleared up. Can we both agree in the future that we'll phone and let the other know if we're going to be late?"
"Sure. Absolutely. Now let's order dinner. And it's on me."
"Wow. That is really gracious of you."

Assertion balanced with caring ensures that there is no critical edge in your voice. You mean what you say, and you are countering the Boaster pattern. The Boaster may not respond positively. What is important is that you are training the Boaster patterned person to consider you a worthwhile person too—a person who is worthy of their attention and admiration.

Handling Someone's Controller Pattern

Here is Jack at work in his office, learning to use his whole Self Compass in diplomatically handling his supervisor's Controller pattern:

Lisa, Jack's project supervisor, stops by his desk. "Jack, have you finished the year-end report yet? I'd like to have a look at it before you send it in."

"Sure, Lisa, I plan to have it done by tomorrow afternoon."

Lisa's eyebrows lift. "Really? That late? What if I have a lot of changes I want you to make? That won't give you the time to do a proper job on it. This report is really important for our funding next year."

Jack feels the tension in his solar plexus. He breathes in, then out, slowly. "Lisa, could you sit down a minute? I need to check out something with you."

Lisa glances at her watch and sighs, "Okay, but make it fast. I've got a meeting soon." She plunks herself down on the chair by Jack's desk.

"It seems to me like you're having trouble trusting me to do a good job on this report. Is that accurate, or am I on the wrong track?"

"Oh, no," Lisa protests, "of course I trust you. It's just that there's so much riding on it."

"Would you feel better if you just took over the project yourself?"

Lisa frowns. "Why? Don't you think you can do the job?"

"I know I can do the job," Jack replies calmly. "I'm skilled in year-end report writing. In order to do a quality job on it, I'll need until tomorrow afternoon. But when you say you think you'll need to do lots of revision, that tells me that you don't share my view that I know what I'm doing." (Notice that Jack is taking his time so that he can deliver a fuller communication to Lisa. This assertion itself keeps her from derailing their talk with a quip and walking away with him under her control.)

Lisa pauses. "Well, of course not. I mean..." She looks flustered. "I do think you can do the job. I'm sure tomorrow afternoon will be fine." She glances at her watch and gets up. "I've got to go." She rushes off.

Jack used his Assertion compass point by standing against Lisa's judgmental attitude and his Love compass point by doing so diplomatically. He used the Strength compass point by affirming his competence and the Weakness compass point by offering to surrender the project to Lisa.

His behavior was Christ-like, because he didn't get aggressive or boastful in his communication with Lisa. Nor did he retreat into resentful compliance and then later gripe about Lisa's micromanaging.

Neutralizing the Power of the Patterns

It will help to keep in mind that these patterns don't exist in isolation. They are interpersonal as well as personal in nature and therefore exert powerful "push-pull" responses from other people. Any given pattern will typically induce a reaction from its opposite compass point. The Worrier pattern, for example, typically pulls the judgmental Controller comeback; the Arguer pattern usually draws the placating response of the Dependent pattern.

Knowing about pattern predictability has its advantages. By pulling back from a situation and seeing it more objectively, you are more likely to recognize these patterns in action and avoid their manipulative traps. By intervening using your whole Self Compass, the patterns lose their hold. Those who are stuck in a particular pattern begin to understand that such manipulation doesn't work, at least not with you.

Reader Moment

This is helpful material, you say. But I suspect it's good to remember that I can't change someone's behavior by my actions.

Crucial point, we say.
Your healthy responses won't provide sufficient momentum for others to change their behavior. This is especially difficult to remember when it involves a

spouse or family member. It is wiser to take responsibility for your own growth and change, in this case, learning to counter manipulation tactfully, whether others choose to change or not.

The good news is that by cleaning up your own side of the communication process, you come to feel more peace about your interactions with others. When you unhook yourself from other people's manipulative patterns, life becomes simpler and more satisfying.

But there is even more good news.

Unexpected though it may be, it is nonetheless true: deep within the rigidity of each personality pattern lies a virtue, ready for the plucking.

What are these virtues? And how do you harvest them, hidden as they are within your Self Compass?

14
SELF COMPASS VIRTUES

You will know them by their fruits.
—Jesus, Mt 7:16

There is a curious paradox rooted in the eight personality patterns. Every one of them possesses a particular virtue unique to that pattern. Yet it is only accessible by embracing your whole Self Compass. If you have been stuck on the Assertion compass point in the Rule-breaker pattern, for example, it is only by embracing the caring of the Love compass point that you reap the virtue of creativity inherent in the Rule-breaker pattern.

Why?

Because true creativity requires caring for others. Without it, creativity deteriorates into manipulative ploys to deceive. But once Rule-breakers reach for the Love compass point, energy used for deception shifts to creative enhancement of other's lives as well as sincere self-expression.

As rigid patterns fall away, in their stead comes the harvest of your labor: Compass virtues. Virtues that can now sprout forth as fruits of the Holy Spirit (Gal 5:22). Why? Because you are surrendering your patterns to the Lord.

The Pleaser and Storyteller patterns yield to the Love compass point virtues of charity and good cheer. The Arguer and Rule-breaker patterns give way to the Assertion compass point virtues of courage and creativity. The Worrier and Loner patterns transform into the Weakness compass point virtues of empathy and objectivity. And the Boaster and Controller patterns find wholeness in the Strength compass point virtues of autonomy and discipline.

Here are the virtues charted on the Self Compass:

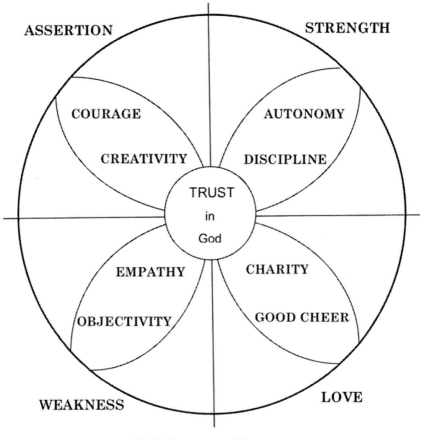

Self Compass Virtues

The rhythmic and self-correcting polarities of Love, Assertion, Weakness and Strength—combined with a deep reliance on Christ—support your transformation from the inside out. Notice how a person's trust in God anchors the center of the Self Compass. Serenity replaces the fear produced by personality patterns when you "trust in the Lord with all your heart" (Prov 3:5).

How do these virtues reveal themselves in actual behavior? What gifts can you expect when you access the LAWS of the Self Compass?

Pleaser—*virtue of charity.*

- Sensitive and sympathetic.
- Doesn't need the limelight.
- A good listener and follower.
- Tender and talented in care for children.
- Quick to forgive.
- Compromises easily.
- Is kind and helpful.

When you diplomatically assert yourself with a family member and feel the ensuing guilt, you employ your whole Self Compass to examine the merits of wallowing in remorse. Acknowledging that the anxiety is difficult to move through (Weakness compass point), you keep on with it anyway (Strength compass point). You decide that you caringly made a necessary point, regardless of the family member's reaction (Love and Assertion compass points). When a peace forms inside, it feels like you're aligned with God's will.

When nurturing other's well-being is combined with the willingness to stand up for your needs and confront unfairness, the capacity for healthy love grows. Intimacy with others moves to deeper levels as redeemed Pleasers now express and handle all feelings—not just "nice" ones.

By exercising the Strength compass point, you develop confidence in your personal power and loving concern for others, realizing that you really count in the world. Instead of automatically disowning compliments, recovering Pleasers are finally comfortable receiving them. You humbly accept your imperfections, knowing that God and others love you as you are.

Storyteller—*virtue of good cheer.*

- ⊕ Makes life exciting, colorful and humorous.
- ⊕ Loves to laugh and play.
- ⊕ Gregarious.
- ⊕ Doesn't take the world too seriously.
- ⊕ Feels lighthearted most of the time.
- ⊕ Always ready for an adventure or surprise.

As a recovering Storyteller, you keep your buoyancy and color, but now, because the Love compass point is balanced with the humility of Weakness, you are sensitive to people's signals that they've heard enough funny stories.

Amazed by the genuine dialogue that ensues, you form relationships with increased depth and feel relaxed even when not in the limelight. Hidden insecurity is replaced by optimistic serenity.

Recovering Storytellers stop to listen to other's points of view. You breathe more fully and speak with a slower delivery so that others are able to take in what you're saying (the Strength compass point in rhythm with Weakness). Time alone, in quiet contemplation or in pursuit of hobbies, grows more enjoyable.

Though you help others feel better with a lively and positive attitude, you acknowledge that it is normal to feel down sometimes. Greater discipline in thinking and decision-making helps tap your intellectual potential (Strength compass point). By developing more confidence and capability, recovering Storytellers no longer feel the need for center stage.

Arguer—*virtue of courage.*

⊕ A master of debate and rhetoric. Not intimidated by anyone.
⊕ Able to hold up under stress.
⊕ Good at confrontation and challenging unfairness.
⊕ A fearless negotiator.

As a recovering Arguer, you shed the angry chip-on-the shoulder and discover what love is all about. Drawing on the virtue of courage, you find ways of asking for forgiveness and making amends to those you have harmed (Love and Weakness compass points). Instead of ventilating explosively when you feel mad, you ask God and others for help in handling anger. Combining caring with the ability to assert, you stand up for other's rights as well as your own.

Recovering Arguers turn suspicion of people's motives into a discerning trust of others. Because your Assertion compass point is balanced by with the Love compass point, you can now upgrade your negotiating skills to include less competitive tension and more concern for overall fairness.

Finding more pleasure in relationships, you laugh or hug more readily. When arguments or emergencies occur, you use the ability to handle stress by holding steady, while working out a solution for the common good.

Rule-breaker—*virtue of creativity.*

⊕ Inventive and imaginative.
⊕ Non-conforming.
⊕ Risk-taking.
⊕ Knows how to cut through red tape.
⊕ Gives novel responses to new or difficult situations.
⊕ Is not intimidated by threats or punishment, which only makes for more resourcefulness.

There comes to be a good feeling about doing the right thing. About researching guidelines for doing tax forms and following them to the letter. About paying for everything you take from a store, even if there's an opportunity not to. About establishing an inner code of conduct where you care about God's opinion of your actions. You like the inner security that comes with having integrity.

When you humbly ask God to be part of your life (Weakness compass point), God can use your creativity to bring innovation and needed changes to the status quo.

Because you are not rule-bound, you can ferret out inventive but workable solutions to problems. A recovering Rule-breaker's sense of adventure and fearlessness allows you to live on the edge where others would fear to tread.

Creativity takes on an altruistic dimension by incorporating empathy from the Weakness compass point with caring service from the Love compass point.

Worrier—*virtue of empathy.*

+ Isn't demanding or competitive.
+ Sensitive rapport with others.
+ Peacemaking.
+ Has a high frustration tolerance.
+ Not motivated by status or material gain.
+ Is especially tender toward children, animals, and those who suffer.

As a recovering Worrier, when you move out of learned helplessness and into the world (Strength compass point), you relate more effectively with people, bringing a much needed virtue to those interactions: empathy for human pain.

It's not that the times of feeling lonely disappear. It's more that when they come, you do something to alleviate them. You actually get yourself to a new church group you've been thinking about checking out. And you stop yourself from disappearing the moment the Bible study is over. You discipline yourself to stay at least five minutes and engage in some sort of conversation. You're good at listening and getting better at talking. Even though it's scary, you're learning to stay with a feeling and express it, rather than avoid it.

Now daring to express needs and wants, you do it in a humble manner, sensitive to the other person's point of view.

Mobilizing your Strength and Assertion compass points brings a depth dimension to the events of your day that before had seemed flat and dreary.

You develop rhythmic access to all four compass points, yet since you favor the Weakness compass point, you are in the enviable position to readily own that you don't have all the answers, and that you need God's help in handling everyday life.

Loner—*virtue of objectivity.*

⊕ Lives and lets live.
⊕ Can be fair-minded and impartial.
⊕ Separates facts from feelings.
⊕ Responds to emergencies with calm detachment.
⊕ Not burdened by other people's expectations.
⊕ Doesn't need to impress anyone.
⊕ Inner-directed.

As a recovering Loner, you move past the pattern's rigidity by touching others—literally. You risk reaching out and touching another human being, in an appropriate context, like a pat on the shoulder of your son; a brush on the cheek of your spouse. Neurons, millions of them, fire in response to this kind of physical contact, providing an emotional connection that strengthens your bond with others. But the recovering Loner perseveres. By learning to breathe and relax, you offer more smiles that let people know you care about them. When they smile back, you feel the enjoyment God intended in creating you.

Jesus understood the importance of sensual contact with others. He fully enjoyed the experience of the woman anointing his feet with expensive oil. He even took the disciples to task for criticizing the expense. So, too, by moving into the Strength and Love compass points, the redeemed Loner finds creative ways to bless others with newfound expressions of love and appreciation.

You learn to bask in the warm glow of a compliment, and feel the pleasure of participating more at work and in family life. Once this process is underway, you bring the virtue of objectivity to human interaction. If a discussion grows overly impassioned, recovering Loners can offer a perspective on the situation unseen by people more emotionally driven. You don't take things personally, so your feedback is honest. By moving into the Assertion compass point, you challenge unfairness toward yourself or others.

Understanding that your primary satisfaction comes from inner-direction, you add to this the emotional payoffs of reaching out to others.

Boaster—*virtue of autonomy.*

+ Self-governing and self-confident.
+ Optimistic.
+ Marches to own tune and not the drumbeat of others.
+ Easily assumes leadership.
+ Takes pride in achievements and personal poise.

There are moments these days when you shake your head in wonder. How didn't you know what you'd been missing? For now the relationship with your sibling holds a tenderness you were unaware was possible. Now a friendship has developed in which the back-and-forth rhythm of communication and communion contributes to another person's happiness as well as your own.

More visits to the Weakness compass point make it is easier to admit limitations, even shortcomings. With the Love compass point engaged, you take the initiative to help those at work join together in common goals. You make it a point to notice and compliment people on their progress, yet maintain authority in your leadership role.

While you appreciate and even assume admiration, you draw much delight from blessing others. You take some flowers to a neighbor who has been ill. You arrange for a baby-sitter so your pastor and his wife can have a night off from caring for their three-month-old baby.

Sometimes you hear a gentle whisper within. A voice that says, "I'm proud of you, my child. And I love you."

Controller—*virtue of discipline.*

- Conscientious, industrious, and reliable.
- Values self-discipline and stick-to-itiveness.
- Endorses social conventions and proprieties.
- Pillar of the community.
- Emphasizes rationality and logic.
- Champion of morality.

What a relief. By enlisting the LAWS of personality, the recovering Controller gets to relax. And play. You find the grimness of constant competence replaced by tasks completed in due time without the need for perfection. You organize yourself to have fun. Going on walks for pleasure as much as exercise, you breathe in the air; listen for the sounds of a bird's song. The fillips of joy floating up from your belly, you realize, come only from letting go.

When you hear that inner judge start up with the old tirades of self-condemnation about how you should have done something better, you stop. *I'm human*, you say. *The planet will carry on without me being perfect.*

Other people become less of an annoyance and more of a gift. You are amazed to discover that when you move into the Weakness compass point and ask for help, others actually do assist you. Caringly. Even efficiently. It shocks you to feel tears in your eyes when this happens. Taking in more deeply that other people love you brings emotional vulnerability. That is uncomfortable. But you are good at persevering, so you allow yourself a degree of surrender, with discernment, to the untidy, not always controllable, world of feelings.

And you begin experiencing what Jesus had in mind when he said, "My peace I give to you; not as the world gives do I give to you. Let not your heart be troubled, neither let it be afraid" (Jn 14:27 NKJV).

Freed to be Your Real Self in Christ

With the infusion of compass virtues, the locus of the self has changed. No longer is it fragmented, imbalanced, stuck on one or more of the compass points. Instead, your personality is now grounded in a balanced, God-oriented center that holds. As the following diagram shows, when you invite God to transform your personality, he dwells in your spiritual core, at the center of your Self Compass.

Instead of predictably patterned behavior, the Self Compass now offers you 360 degrees of choice to use as appropriate for any given situation. Now you are freed to utilize these virtues, expressed through your own individual style in Christ. Precious in his eyes, there is no one else like you, because "the very hairs of your head are all numbered" (Mt 10:30 NKJV).

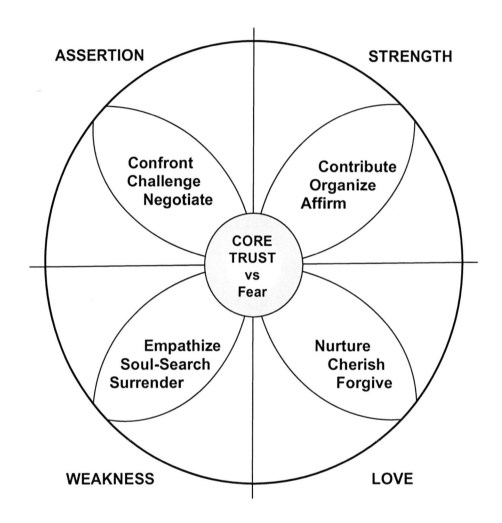

Compass Living

How comforting to know there is a compass of right-eousness that clearly defines growth and wholeness in the Lord. Jesus says, "Those who do what is true come to the light, so that it may be clearly seen that their deeds have been done in God" (Jn 3:21).

Reader Moment

I like the health and hope embedded in this diagram, you say. A Self Compass that helps me love God and others as I love myself.

Well said! we reply.

The Self Compass, anchored in Christ's own personality, and upheld by modern science, provides daily answers to personality and relationship needs in the trenches of daily life.

A Christian growth tool that really works.

Appendix: Compass Theory Research

The theoretical underpinnings of the Compass Model derive from research at the Institute of Personality Assessment in Berkeley conducted by Leary et al and summarized in the classic book, *Interpersonal Diagnosis of Personality: A Functional Theory and Methodology for Personality Evaluation* (New York: The Ronald Press, 1957). The factor analysis of personality traits in a sample of over five thousand cases revealed that two polarities form the core of personality.

Dr. Dan Montgomery and his colleague Dr. Everett L. Shostrom labeled these two polarities Love/Assertion and Weakness/Strength. (Everett L. Shostrom and Dan Montgomery, *Healing Love: How God Works Within the Personality* [Nashville, TN: Abingdon Press, 1979]; *God In Your Personality* [Nashville, TN: Abingdon Press, 1986]; *The Manipulators*, [Nashville, TN: Abingdon Press, 1990].

Personality research symbolizing the self as a circle divided into four quadrants began over a hundred years ago. Since then, researchers have variously referred to this model as:

⊕ The mandala (Carl G. Jung, *Man and His Symbols* [Laurel, 1968]).

⊕ The actualizing model (Everett L. Shostrom, *Actualizing Therapy* [San Diego, CA: Edits Pub., 1976]); (Lawrence M. Brammer, Everett L. Shostrom, and Philip J. Abrego, *Therapeutic Psychology* [Englewood Cliffs, New Jersey: Prentice-Hall, Inc., 1993, 1989, 1982, 1977, 1968, 1960]).

⊕ The interpersonal circle (Donald J. Kiesler, *Contemporary Interpersonal Theory and Research: Personality, Psychopathology, and Psychotherapy* [New York: John Wiley and Sons, 1996]); (Lorna Smith Benjamin, *Interpersonal Diagnosis and Treatment of Personality Disorders, Second Edition* [New York: The Guilford Press, 1996]).

⊕ The circumplex model (Robert Plutchik and Hope R. Conte, *Circumplex Models of Personality and Emotions* [Washington, D.C.: American Psychological Association, 1997]).

The Self Compass® growth tool, developed by Dr. Montgomery, resembles a physical compass. Its circle represents the boundary that separates every person from the world and denotes a person's unique identity over the lifespan. The quadrants represent dynamics at work within each person.

Compass theory, then, obtains its name from the assumption that the compass-like integration of complementary opposites contributes to psychological and spiritual wholeness.

The Self Compass supports a health-oriented psychology, while simultaneously accounting for most of the personality disorders found in the *Diagnostic and Statistical Manual of Mental Disorders*. Dan and Kate Montgomery have developed a psychospiritual model for growth and transformation in *Compass Psychotheology: Where Psychology and Theology Really Meet* (Compass Works, 2006).

Over six hundred studies in clinical, educational, and religious settings have corroborated the growth psychology that undergirds the Self Compass growth tool.

These studies include M. B. Freedman, 1985; Freedman, Leary, Ossario, & Coffey, 1951; Shostrom, 1963, 1964, 1970, 1972, 1978; Shostrom & Knapp, 1966; Shostrom & Riley, 1968; Shostrom, Knapp, & Knapp, 1976; LaForge, 1977, 1985; LaForge, Freedman, & Wiggins, 1985; LaForge, Leary, Naboisek, Coffey, & Freedman, 1954; LaForge and Suczek, 1955; Leary, 1955, 1957; Leary & Coffey, 1954, 1955; Leary & Harvey, 1956; Leary, Lane, Apfelbaum, Croppa, & Kaufmann, 1956; Strack, 1996; Wiggins, 1985; Carson, 1969; Anchim & Kiesler, 1982; Kiesler, 1988; Safran & Segal, 1990; Andrews, 1991; Benjamin, 1993.

The application of the Self Compass to counseling and therapy is called Compass Therapy (Dan Montgomery, *Christian Counseling That Really Works: Compass Therapy In Action* [Compass Works, 2006]).

Raymond Corsini, considered by many as the dean of American counseling and psychotherapy, has called Dr. Montgomery's approach to counseling "the therapeutic system of the future." (*Handbook on Innovative Therapy, Second Edition* [New York: John Wiley and Sons, 2001, 1981]).

SELF COMPASS READERS GROUP GUIDE

For group discussions to enjoy success, interpersonal guidelines for sharing are an important prerequisite. We recommend that participants understand the need for confidentiality, which is the life-blood of self-disclosure and trust. Individuals are free to express personal experiences about their own lives, but withhold comments about others. The goal is to develop a warm interpersonal climate free from criticism. Group discussion leaders can trust the group process and the presence of God to draw people out and encourage healing growth.

Discussion Questions

1. How do you think Jesus showed Love balanced with Assertion in the Gospel accounts? What actions does he take that show he loved himself as well as others?

2. How does Christ display the characteristics of the Servant Leader, balancing the compass points of healthy Weakness and Strength.

3. What does "sin" mean in the context of the Self Compass? Why are personality patterns harmful?

4. The Self Compass shows where you are stuck and how to take "growth stretches" that lead to greater wholeness. What are the advantages to personality development? What are the advantages to compass living vs. patterned behavior?

5. It can be both uncomfortable and a relief when you discover the results of your Self Compass Inventory. What was your reaction? Why do you think it wise to discern a person or group's trustworthiness before discussing the results with anyone else?

6. When the Love compass point is exaggerated, too much love makes people compliant (Pleaser) or attention craving (Storyteller). How are these patterns alike? How do they differ? How do you react when you are with someone stuck in the Pleaser pattern? What strategies have you found that work when buttonholed by a Storyteller patterned person?

7. When the Assertion compass point is exaggerated, too much assertion results in making people argumentative (Arguer), or exploitive (Rule-breaker). What does it feel like to be with someone stuck in the Arguer pattern? How does a Rule-breaker patterned person use charm to deceive you? How can you counter someone who is trying to manipulate you in these ways?

8. When the Weakness compass point is exaggerated, too much weakness results in making
people withdrawn (Worrier) or detached (Loner).
How would you characterize the experiences you
have had with someone stuck in the Worrier pattern? How can you tell when a Loner patterned
person is beginning to grow out of this pattern?

9. When the Strength compass point is exaggerated,
too much strength makes people compulsive
(Controller) or arrogant (Boaster). Do you agree
with the Montgomerys that the Controller pattern is the most subtle of all these personality
patterns? Why or why not? How is the Boaster
pattern different from the Controller pattern?
How is it different from the Storyteller pattern?

9. How is it that a pattern's virtues only bear fruit
when you are outgrowing the pattern and moving
toward a balanced Self Compass?

10. By pulling back from a situation and seeing it
more objectively, you are more likely to recognize
patterns in action and avoid their manipulative
traps. How does the Self Compass help you neu-
tralize people's patterns? How does it make your
own behavior more creative?

11. Why is it important not to be seduced into thinking that your healthy responses will provide
sufficient momentum for others to change their
behavior?

12. How is your behavior changing as you apply the Self Compass to your personality and relationships?

13. How does the Self Compass increase your accuracy in interpreting other people's behavior?

14. In what ways have you drawn closer to Christ as a result of your personality growth? Are there moments when you're aware of guidance from the Holy Spirit?

15. What compass growth goals are you still working on in your relationships with your family and co-workers?

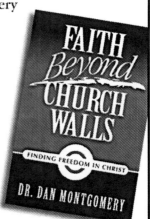

Printed in the United States
85350LV00011B/53/A